# Who's in Your Room?

## The Question That Will Change Your Life

### SECOND EDITION

**STEWART EMERY** AND **IVAN MISNER**
WITH **DOUG HARDY**

## BK

Berrett–Koehler Publishers, Inc.

Berrett-Koehler Publishers, Inc.
1333 Broadway, Suite 1000
Oakland, CA 94612-1921
Tel: (510) 817-2277
Fax: (510) 817-2278
www.bkconnection.com

ORDERING INFORMATION

**Quantity sales.** Special discounts are available on quantity purchases by corporations, associations, and others. For details, contact the "Special Sales Department" at the Berrett-Koehler address above.
**Individual sales.** Berrett-Koehler publications are available through most bookstores. They can also be ordered directly from Berrett-Koehler: Tel: (800) 929-2929; Fax: (802) 864-7626; www.bkconnection .com.
**Orders for college textbook / course adoption use.** Please contact Berrett-Koehler: Tel: (800) 929-2929; Fax: (802) 864-7626.

Distributed to the U.S. trade and internationally by Penguin Random House Publisher Services.

Berrett-Koehler and the BK logo are registered trademarks of Berrett-Koehler Publishers, Inc.

Printed in the United States of America

Berrett-Koehler books are printed on long-lasting acid-free paper. When it is available, we choose paper that has been manufactured by environmentally responsible processes. These may include using trees grown in sustainable forests, incorporating recycled paper, minimizing chlorine in bleaching, or recycling the energy produced at the paper mill.

Library of Congress Cataloging-in-Publication Data

Names: Emery, Stewart, 1941- author. | Misner, Ivan R., 1956- author. |
    Hardy, Doug, author.
Title: Who's in your room? the question that will change your life / by
    Stewart Emery and Ivan Misner, with Doug Hardy.
Description: Revised and updated, second edition. | Oakland, CA :
    Berrett-Koehler Publishers, [2023] | Includes bibliographical references
    and index.
Identifiers: LCCN 2022023120 (print) | LCCN 2022023121 (ebook) | ISBN
    9781523002122 (paperback) | ISBN 9781523002139 (pdf) | ISBN
    9781523002146 (epub) | ISBN 9781523002153 (electronic)
Subjects: LCSH: Interpersonal relations. | Interpersonal conflict. |
    Self-realization.
Classification: LCC BF724.3.I58 E44 2023 (print) | LCC BF724.3.I58
    (ebook) | DDC 158.2—dc23/eng/20220729
LC record available at https://lccn.loc.gov/2022023120
LC ebook record available at https://lccn.loc.gov/2022023121

Second Edition
29 28 27 26 25 24 23 22    10 9 8 7 6 5 4 3 2 1

Book producer: PeopleSpeak
Text designer: Reider Books
Cover designer: Adam Johnson
Doug Hardy's photo: Pierre Chiha

*To all of you who embrace self-authorship of your life.*
*Living the quest for the best version of yourself in the company*
*of others who are likewise engaged is the purpose of this book.*

# Contents

# You Become Whom You Are With

"IMAGINE THAT you live your entire life in just one room."

We have introduced this idea to thousands of people over the years, and they have been amazed at the power such a simple concept has for reshaping their lives. Many immediately have an OMG moment as they visualize their rooms. Some people's rooms are spacious and welcoming, while others are ominous and chaotic. Some people launch into flashback mode and say that for them the idea feels like watching a high-speed rerun of their entire lives. Some see a metaphorical train wreck; others see the need for a bit more clarity to focus on the best parts of their rooms. After that first visualization, nearly everyone asks us how they can expand the initial idea into a practical framework for improving their lives.

Our relationships are our lives, and in a very real sense, you become whom you are with. Your feelings, interactions, beliefs, inward life, and outward ambitions are shaped by the people you invite into your life. Just as important, the quality of your relationships depends on how you manage them, for better and worse.

*Who's in Your Room?* offers a method for understanding all the relationships in your life with clarity and courage. Although the question is simple—in fact, *because* the question is simple—it possesses an unlimited capacity to be applied to the details of anyone's life, including yours.

By consciously choosing which people occupy your psychological room and where they are, you gain tremendous power to create the life you want. Merging the discoveries of brain science with the insights of modern psychology and ancient philosophy, *Who's in Your Room?* is a tool of unlimited usefulness for taking control of your life.

In this book, you will learn the following skills:

- How to see all the relationships in your life as your conscious and unconscious minds view them
- How to create a definition of *relationship* that is meaningful to you
- How to detect the ways people with whom you have relationships—living or dead, physically near and far—influence your thoughts, emotions, and actions
- How to understand the ways people interact in your room
- How to choose who gets in, what they bring with them, and who stays out
- How to direct people to the right places in your room, whether near or far from you
- How to handle the people who are already in your room and the people who want to enter
- How to deal with difficult people forcing their way toward you
- How to say no without sounding like a jerk

This book presents a highly effective process for choosing who is in your room. We've included practical exercises (marked by an arrow ➤) for shaping the best room for your own values and your life's purpose—in other words, living the life you've always wanted. Throughout the book we'll share stories of people who have used the question at critical moments in their lives to clarify their situations about love, friendship, money, business, difficult people, and how they spend, in the words of a friend, "all the breaths they have left." At the end of each chapter, we'll include a longer story of a person we know who asked, "Who's in my room?" to great effect in different situations. (For the sake of simplicity, we will adopt the copyeditor Benjamin Dreyer's suggestion to embrace the twenty-first-century *they* to refer to nonspecific people. Like Dreyer, we grew up using the universal *he*. Like him, we're not too old to change.)

In each chapter you'll also find quick tips and observations we've made through many years of working with people to help them take control of their rooms. Those are labeled "Rules of the Room."

The question "Who's in your room?" has been used by people from all walks of life who have different goals, values, dreams, and ambitions. It's been used by new graduates and retirees and people of every age in between. It's helped people achieve better emotional and mental health, greater clarity about their goals, and healthier relationships of all kinds. People tell us they relate and adapt the stories in this book to their own life circumstances, and it has made their lives better in too many ways to count.

This method works from this moment forward. You will begin to treat constraining elements from your past with a new understanding of how to relate to people in the future.

Yes, it's that powerful.

We know the effectiveness of this simple metaphor because we have spent our lives helping people make better choices. Stewart Emery is one of the founders of the modern human potential movement. For decades he has helped people take back their power. He is an entrepreneur, executive coach, and leader who has led thousands of employees and hundreds of managers through the vision, values, strategy, and leadership initiatives based on research from the international bestsellers *Built to Last*, *Good to Great*, and *Success Built to Last*. He has been awarded a doctor of humane letters degree from John F. Kennedy University. Ivan Misner is the founder and chief visionary officer of Business Network International (BNI), the world's largest business networking organization, whose members generate millions of referrals and billions of dollars in business yearly. At the core of BNI's principles is the joy of people succeeding by helping each other. CNN called Ivan the "Father of Modern Networking." He is a *New York Times* bestselling author of twenty-two books. Doug Hardy worked as an editor in book, magazine, and internet publishing for forty years. He has written and collaborated on eighteen books and hundreds of articles, with a special focus on human capital issues (meaning people at work) and on ways to build sustainable, growing, and human-centered organizational cultures.

Throughout our careers, we've returned to the perennial truth that all our lives are made up of relationships, for better or worse, and that by waking up to the truth of our relationships, we can choose for the better.

*Who's in Your Room?* is an invitation to choose both a better life and a path that will lead you there. For years we have tested many ideas springing from this simple metaphor, and this book collects those that have had the greatest meaning to the thousands who have tried them. It's a road-tested way of making your life better. The answers will inform and transform every aspect of your life. You can and will discover how. This is not just our promise to you; it can be your promise to yourself.

# 1

# Imagine You Live
# in This Room

IMAGINE THAT you live your entire life in one room. Inside are all the people with whom you have ever had a relationship, including their temperaments, histories, and personalities. The room is infinitely large. You can update and expand your room to accommodate new people and new possibilities in your life. You can design your room any way you like.

Your room has a unique and permanent feature, however. It has only one door. It will only *ever* have one door. You may think that there is nothing unusual about that; lots of rooms have only one door. True, but this particular door is a one-way door. ENTER ONLY, NO EXIT. Whoever comes through this door, and whatever you let them bring in, cannot leave—ever. They and their baggage will be with you in your room for the rest of your life.

This concept matters to you because the quality of your life depends on who's in your room.

One more time: *the quality of your life depends on who's in your room.*

The person you become and whether or not you are happy and successful is profoundly influenced by who's in your room. Whether you achieve harmony and fulfillment in your life depends on how you handle the people in your room.

Pause for a moment. How is this idea landing for you?

Who's in your room? Close your eyes and look around with your mind. Take a quick inventory. You could start with your family and friends, your business partners, neighbors, and people who show up frequently in your social media feed. Who's up close and personal? Who else is in there—people you work with, people you love having in your room, or people you wish weren't there?

Based on what you've seen so far, ask yourself, Would I have made different choices about whom to let into my room, and whom to keep out, had I known that anybody who came in was going to be there forever? Almost everyone we've asked has said yes to this question.

Once you recognize this point, you have two important questions going forward: How are you going to select people you wish to have in your room now that you know they can never leave? And how will you deal with the people who are already there?

At this point, some folks push back on the original premise: "It can't literally be true that once people get in my room they are in it forever!" they say. But even though you don't physically live in a single room, the psychological truth is that they *are* in your metaphorical room forever. In fact, neurologists report that as far as your brain is concerned, the metaphor is quite real. According to Dr. Daniel Amen, founder of the Amen Clinics, significant input that is received in your brain triggers neural activity that cannot simply be erased or deleted as though it never happened.

If someone hurts you, is mean to you, or belittles you, they stay in your room, and their fingerprints are all over your brain. Their voice is in the voice-recognition parts of your brain's temporal lobe, their face is in the facial-recognition parts, and their behavior is in your memory. When you meet someone and they get anchored in there, they don't go away. Consciously or unconsciously, people may be out of your life, but they're still in your head. The things they say and do affect your thinking, behavior, and experience—forever.

You might, for example, believe you have ended a relationship, terminated a project, or let a previous commitment go, but these events have left an indelible mark—affecting your future experience in myriad ways—for better or worse, whether you like it or not.

Do you have dreams about people who aren't in your life anymore? According to your subconscious mind, they *are* in your life. When we say "That dream felt so real!" we're stating a psychological fact of life. When you dream of being back at the lakeside with that grandparent you loved, the dreaming mind is telling you that they are in some way still alive and it's always summer at that lakeside.

This realization is one of those good news/bad news deals because, to our good fortune, it's not just about the troublemakers. This is also the case when someone genuinely loves you, praises you, or skillfully mentors you. Your mean sibling is in there, but so is your loving grandparent.

Your past is archived in your psyche, just as your future will also be when it unfolds to become a part of your past. What's done is done. The events of the past cannot be undone. An action taken is final. A word uttered cannot be unsaid.

## What Is a Relationship?

One of the perennial questions we hear when doing this work is "What do you mean by a relationship?" It's one of those words that means different things to different people. A dictionary definition is "the way in which people are connected." Another is "the quality of connection." For the purposes of this book, we invite you to consider exactly what a relationship means to you. Keep an open mind because we will continuously challenge you to think deeply about every relationship you have and make decisions based on that. Continue to question what energy is flowing between you and each person in your room. Is it positive, negative, or, as usually happens in life, a dynamic and changeable mixture of both?

Do you ever remember doing something you regret from long ago and cringe in response? We know a person who, as a child, joined a gang in bullying the new kid at school. Now a middle-aged man, he literally cringes and mutters, "I'm sorry!" when he remembers that moment. (If his wife is nearby, she asks, "For what?") Great actors have used this cringe reaction as a tool: by deeply remembering times they were sad or embarrassed or joyously in love, they inhabit those emotions long after the incidents that produced them. The psychological reality that the unconscious remembers and revisits emotions as real is the heart of many great performances and a key to method acting. We suspect you have many such happy and not-so-happy memories.

We are who we are because of and in spite of others. Moving forward, you can carefully choose who and what comes into your room and into your life. Choose well, and you will love your life. Don't choose well, and you know how *that* goes! The good news is that throughout this book we'll show you how to make better choices that will dramatically improve your happiness. When you design your room intentionally, you transform your life.

This mindset is all about looking forward to the future. It's not about looking back in anguish to the past.

## Start with a Look Around

In her influential book *Mindset: The New Psychology of Success,* psychologist Carol Dweck posed the essential finding that individuals who have a "growth mindset" are better able to overcome setbacks than those with a "fixed mindset." In Dweck's framing, a growth mindset means a belief that intelligence can be developed over time, and a fixed mindset is the belief that intelligence is predetermined. To simplify her insight, these points of view shape whether someone views setbacks and failures as a challenge to be overcome (growth mindset) or as an innate and unchanging lack of ability (fixed mindset).

Your room is a way to adopt a growth mindset with relationships you might think will never change. However much it seems that your present is predetermined by all the people you've known and the baggage they've brought into your room, you can decide today how much that limits your ability to grow and change and become more conscious of the choices you make for living your life.

The best place to start is the here and now. Putting the transformative power of "Who's in your room?" to work begins with an inquiry rather than a rush to action. For this review of how your daily experience is being shaped by the people in your room, we're going to ask you to engage your imagination and play along a little—maybe more than a little. You can start with something familiar you say about your life.

For example, perhaps your life is chaotic. Every day seems to bring a new crisis, and you want to change that. But is chaos a cause or an effect? In other words, does chaos name the disease, or is it merely a symptom? (*Disease* might seem too strong a word. However, when you remember that *disease* derives from the *absence of ease*, then it surely applies to this state of affairs.)

Looking around the room that is your life, you will likely see people who gained entry carrying the curse of chaos with them. You know who we're talking about—people who don't feel they are alive unless they're immersed in drama. When you look around your room, do you see people spray-painting graffiti on your walls? Are they pushing others out of the way as they jockey for the best position? You might even have become one of those people, which can happen when you stay too long around such energy. The chaotic life has you living in an overcrowded room. Too many people, too much stuff, too many obligations, too little time—and all of it feels *very urgent*.

What if those people were a bit farther away in your room, say, toward the back where they can't nudge you constantly with their Very Important Issue? You don't hear them demanding your attention quite so much, and even though they can never leave, their example of chaos looks less compelling from a distance.

Does your life seem harsh and angry, perhaps not all the time but sometimes? Recall a specific time when you experienced harshness and anger. It helps to recount a memory that comes up a lot. Put yourself back in that moment. Who's in your room with you? Notice whether you have a harsh and angry person in your presence—perhaps several harsh and angry people or even a mob.

On the other hand, imagine your life is filled with love and kindness. Next, recall a time when your experience felt like a flood of human warmth and positivity swirling around you and washing over you and your room was filled with light. Notice who's in your room with you.

Your experience in each of these examples is driven by either resonance or dissonance.

## Who's Plucking Your Strings?

In physics, resonance is a phenomenon that occurs when a vibrating system or external force drives another system to oscillate at a specific preferential frequency. Imagine two pianos side by side in a room. If you hit the middle C key on one piano while someone presses the sustain pedal on the other one, the middle C string will vibrate on the second piano *without its key being struck*. The second piano's string picks up sound waves from the air that have its natural frequency, and it responds. This is resonance at work.

Carry that over to the human mind and spirit and you understand why we say we resonate with certain people. Some of their qualities and behaviors cause us to respond positively, often with the same qualities.

In contrast, there's dissonance. An example of dissonance almost all of us have experienced is the harsh, disagreeable sound fingernails can make when scratching a chalkboard. Our ears and brains are predisposed to dislike that frequency (two thousand to four thousand hertz). Emotionally, we experience dissonance when we become subjected to inconsistencies between a person's actions and their stated values. Our minds and emotions crave consistency. (Another example most of us have experienced is being hurt by the behavior of a person who professed to love us.)

We human beings are like those piano strings. Some of us are even described as being high-strung. Resonance is an agreeable sensation, but dissonance is not. You've heard of someone's buttons being pushed; that would be a moment of dissonance. When you experienced this yourself, you probably showed signs that certain people and situations were pushing your buttons and that you'd rather avoid them.

Your buttons aren't exactly being pushed but rather your emotional strings are picking up energy from others' emotional strings—sometimes intensely. Sometimes this feels good (resonance) and other times not so much (dissonance).

The point here is that you are, metaphorically speaking, a multistringed work of art in progress. Who's in your room has everything to do with the emotional, intellectual, physical, and spiritual strings resonating within you. You will probably express many of these vibrations externally, such as when you see someone you love, you light up and welcome them warmly. On the other hand, if you see a person you don't care for or trust, you are likely to avoid them and the unpleasant inner experience of dissonance.

## Waking Up to Your Inner Reality

Sometimes we are unaware of the internal experience that triggers our behavior. This is particularly the case when we suddenly become angry. It can happen abruptly, and we are in reaction mode before being conscious of what triggered that feeling. What can be unconscious to us can be blindingly obvious to other people, which can be a catalyst for all kinds of misunderstandings and grief. Developing self-awareness can help significantly. You can become skilled at identifying the inner experiences of resonance and dissonance and then consciously choose how to behave in any given moment.

If you take the time to contemplate your life, you will notice themes as you identify the relationships you have with the people in your room and all the obligations that came in with them. Allow yourself to become aware of how all these aspects influence you and your daily experience. This process is not about establishing blame or fault—doing so serves no useful purpose—but rather noticing resonance and dissonance as a guide to where you can invest more time and how you can manage your room. Resonance and dissonance tip you off to those relationships in which you are living authentically, resonating with people, and those in which you are enduring that fingernails-on-a-chalkboard feeling.

Hospice nurse Bronnie Ware witnessed the last days of dying patients with compassion and kindness for years. In her bestseller *The Top Five Regrets of the Dying*, she observed that the number one regret people have when death is closing in on them is "I wish I'd had the courage to live a life true to myself, not the life others expected of me."

Why do so many people come to the end of their lives carrying this regret? Their attention was focused for a lifetime on other people's expectations, demands, needs, cravings, dreams, frustrations, and desires. To return to the string metaphor, they spent their lives trying to resonate with other instruments without playing their own.

Your room is filled with people from your past and present. Some are sources of resonance, and some create only dissonance. Most do some of both. If your conscious and unconscious attention is focused most of the time on fulfilling those expectations and needs, you'll end up with that number one regret Ware identified.

---

## Rules of the Room

We compare our insides to other people's outsides. Sometimes people show us only what they want us to see of their outside. If we buy into that superficial picture, we'll always assume people are more confident, brave, smart, sophisticated, or so on than us. We feel our shortcomings and fears acutely—but everybody has them, even if we haven't seen a particular person's inner life. It takes time to know more about who they really are.

---

The theologian and social critic Howard Thurman counseled, "Don't ask what the world needs. Ask what makes you come alive and go do it. Because what the world needs are people who have come alive."

One cautionary note as you explore and take control of your room in the following chapters: we are in no way suggesting you don't share yourself with and extend yourself to others. That's the essence of love. We believe that your life will change for the better as you see your room more and more clearly and make conscious choices about who you let in.

As for the metaphorical versus actual idea of a room, instead of asking whether the room is a physical or mental construct, ask yourself, What if I were willing, from this moment on, to live as though it *were* true? *You* are the architect of your emotional, mental, spiritual, and physical room. You need to craft an environment filled with resonance rather than dissonance. Build a room that makes you come alive because the room always wins.

## Visualize Your Room

▶ This exercise can be done in stages. If you're familiar with other visualization techniques, feel free to adapt to your preferred method. We suggest a combination of visualizing with your eyes closed and writing down what you "see" afterward. As you proceed through the exercises in this book, you might return to this visualization to understand how your room changes over time. This room is infinitely adjustable, so you don't have to get it "right" the first time!

Here's one other detail that might help you visualize this fascinating room that is your life: your room is not yet full. Your room has no maximum capacity. There's room for more people in it—such as people who can mentor you to achieve the life you want. The question for you is, Who do you want to attract into your room?

You can do this visualization more than once, and have some fun with it. Ivan is often asked in live presentations where the room is. He points to one side of his head and says, "It starts here," then points to the other side and says, "And it ends here!" Stewart tells people that, if they like, their room can be sitting on a magic carpet that takes them to Times Square; Aspen, Colorado; or a tropical island. It's up to you.

1.  Choose a quiet place where you won't be disturbed for at least twenty minutes. Close your eyes and relax. If you know relaxation exercises or meditation, take a few minutes to center yourself. Pay attention to your breath moving in and out of your body.
2.  Imagine your room. Make it as clear as possible and see yourself there. You might think of it as a simple empty room, a beach, or a canyon that can be accessed through only one door. Your room might change physically over time, but—whatever its physical appearance—the basic principles will never change: one door, and once people are in, they never leave.

3.  Then imagine the people in your room. See the people with whom you have a meaningful relationship today. See the people with whom you've had a strong relationship in the past. Give this some time; who is nearby and who is far away? You don't have to remember everyone in this first visualization. People have a way of showing up later. Remember, there's room for everyone.

4.  Choose one or two people who are most important to you. They might be a life partner, parent, grandparent, sibling, or business partner. They might be close friends from the present or past. Think about them as vividly as possible—their faces, the clothes they wear, the sound of their voices.

5.  For each person, consider your relationship. Think more deeply than simple words. How does this person make you feel when they are nearby? Take your time to explore your feelings fully. What is the resonance or dissonance you feel?

6.  At the end of the visualization, write the names of as many people in your room as you wish. Note where they were in the room—close or far, in light or shadow. Note their demeanor and whether they told you anything. If you like, draw your room or write down its physical characteristics. You might want to use a notebook or binder because you'll return to this room many times.

Actually, you won't "return" to this room—because nobody leaves, including you.

# Are You Even in Your Room?
## Joanie's Story Part I

*Joanie is Joan Emery, Stewart's wife. He's had the opportunity to watch her closely as she works with people, acting as counselor, coach, and cheerleader as they travel forward on the journey of their life. She believes that committing to waking up in your room as perfectly you and carefully living the question "Who's in your room?" is the most powerful transformational practice you can embrace.*

I was getting into bed one night when I was five or six years old. In front of my bed were three or four shelves. Piled high on the shelves were stuffed animals and dolls.

One of my dolls caught my eye, and I decided I wanted to bring her into bed with me, so I got out of bed, picked up my doll, climbed back in, and started to cuddle her. I was about to close my eyes and happily drift off to sleep when my eye caught another doll, and I thought, "Well, maybe I'll bring this doll with me to bed too," so I got out of bed again, collected the doll, and got back under the covers. I had these two dolls with me in bed when suddenly one of my favorite stuffed animals caught my eye, and I thought, "Well, I could bring my stuffed animal to bed too." This all went on for quite some time until my bed was piled high with all the dolls and stuffed animals from each of the shelves, and I was trying to get to sleep on the floor.

A little while later my dad came in to check on me. He saw my bed piled high with all of the stuffed animals and dolls and said, "Joan, what are you doing?" I remember saying to my dad, "I didn't want anyone to feel left out, so I just started one at a time to bring all of my animals and dolls to bed." My dad looked at me and said, "But Joan, you're sleeping on the floor because now there's no room left for you!"

This memory has had such an impact on me because I think that today in my life I make so much room for everybody else that it often feels like there's no room left for me. I was not in my own room. Even if I managed to squeeze my way into my own room, oftentimes it was not the real me who made it in.

Ever since I started living with the idea of Who's in your room? my journey of discovery has accelerated. The first insight was that I never want anybody to feel left out or excluded because I don't want to feel left out or excluded. The next insight was that I noticed I always tend to have a crowd in my room, including people I don't particularly like, because I want so much to be liked. This feels like a downward spiral.

Even if it seems as if people like me, I have no idea which me they really like. Do they like the me that pretends to be whatever they need me to be so they will like me, or do they actually like the real me hiding under all the pretense? On a positive note, I discovered that whenever I caught myself doing this, in that moment I could choose to behave differently and grow toward freedom as a result.

Now I have stopped doing the things that I've done to be liked. I keep going deeper and deeper. It is like I am going down a staircase, and I keep uncovering things. I have always been making choices based on the consideration of what people will think of me rather than choosing something because it is deeply meaningful to me.

Although by now it feels like another lifetime, I spent over five years working in the film industry when I was in my twenties, beginning with a year and a half in New York as a production assistant on *The Godfather*, then over to complete the production in Sicily, where I was invited to move to Rome and continue working in the movie business.

When I finally arrived back in California five years later, I soon felt like I didn't fit in anywhere. Nothing seemed or felt real, especially me. In Italy I felt alive. Back home, I felt empty inside—more so at night. I met a man named Pete Cameron, whom I talked to about my struggle, and he handed me a paper napkin upon which was written "You don't have to be perfect, just be perfectly you." My heart took a little leap of joy. What if this was actually true? Soon after, I attended an Actualizations workshop given by a man called Stewart Emery.

I went to that workshop more than thirty-five years ago, and while no one was asking "Who's in your room?" way back then, a core idea of the workshop was that if you wanted to change your life, you had to keep the company of people committed to changing their own. I put this idea into practice and developed a whole new set of friendships among fellow travelers on the journey to becoming a fully integrated, fully alive, freely choosing human being.

In retrospect, I have now been practicing the idea contained in the question "Who's in your room?" for over half my life. What a difference this has made. I have a lot more space for me in my room these days.

What I found is that for the power of "Who's in your room?" to be available to you, you also have to ask yourself, Am I really in my room? The answer is yes only if it is your true self who is in your room.

The room idea can be transforming, self-nurturing, and even healing. This can be especially true when not all the people you let into your room turn out to be the nice ones. Joanie tells another story about the joys and pitfalls of her room in chapter 8.

# 2

# The Most Important
# People in Your Room

AS YOU BECOME more familiar with your room, we'd like to introduce the two most important people there. They are different from everyone else, because unlike everyone else, they are completely under your control. They are 100 percent on your side, and they're not distracted by hidden agendas or divided loyalties. Think of them as lifelong companions going forward from this moment; they are the people who give you power over your room and thus over other people in your life.

They are the *doorkeeper* and the *concierge*, and they are entirely your creation. That doesn't make them fake, however. As your creation they can be just as real to your subconscious mind as all the flesh-and-blood people whom you've let into your room. They are not made of molecules, but don't let that little physical fact detract from their power.

Put simply, the doorkeeper gives people permission to enter your room (where, please remember, they never leave). The concierge has the power to direct people where to go in your room—whether they are close to you or far away and whether they move freely around or are allowed to remain in only one place. Their actions are simple, but put them to work and you'll find they are among the best friends you have ever had.

Envision your doorkeeper and concierge in the way most comfortable to you. Male or female, tall or short, a twin of Whoopi Goldberg or Natalie Portman, the doppelgänger of Javier Bardem or Danny DeVito—it's up to you. That includes their dress: if you want your doorkeeper in a double-breasted blue uniform coat and your concierge in a toga, go for it. Take some time in the visualizations below to find images that work for you.

Ultimately, the rules you establish with your doorkeeper and concierge directly relate to how you want to live and what you hope to achieve. They also have a substantive influence on all those things that make you, well, *you*—whether you're popular or lonely, whether you're liked or disliked, whether you attract good opportunities or not, whether you're accelerating or decelerating in life, whether you have enriching relationships or meaningless ones with people who take advantage of you, whether you're married to your soul mate or not, whether you live in a cluttered trailer or the home of your dreams, whether you're happy or depressed, whether you're in debt or financially sound, whether you enjoy or hate your job, whether you shoulder the weight of too much stress or not, and so on.

## The Doorkeeper

Consider the door to your room. There it sits, closed but not locked, ready to swing open when the next person pushes their way in. When you're young, you can only sit and marvel at the parade of people who come through it into your room. It takes a few years before you begin to understand that not all the people who come in are ones you necessarily want in the room.

Even after you figure out the meaning and function of that door, you have to spend some time learning how and when and why you should use it. Until you reach that stage in your life, the door swings wide open at the slightest touch.

You begin to wonder whether there is a way to control who comes in through the door. We are here to tell you that there is. You can, in fact, take control over when that door opens and when it stays shut.

Imagine your doorkeeper as someone who intimately knows everything about you and will act as your guardian from now on. Your doorkeeper is clear about your personal values and what matters to you. They know what you are deeply passionate about and are committed to supporting the best in you. Your doorkeeper will not let anybody into the room of your life who does not support your values, your passions, what has meaning to you, and the best in you.

You must remember that the doorkeeper cannot prevent outside events from happening. The stock market might crash—and your doorkeeper can still keep out the people who exploit your fear of financial insecurity. A pandemic might sweep the world—and your doorkeeper can tell the people who want you to engage in risky behaviors to stay out.

Of course, you do have to brief your doorkeeper before they go to work. Your doorkeeper needs from you a set of values and guidelines that they will use to determine who, or what, is allowed to enter into the room of your life or business. This means you have to get really clear about your values and what matters to you. You need to recognize what it is you are deeply passionate about and make a commitment to the best in you. Until you do, you will not be able to tell the difference between an opportunity and a distraction.

If you've never clearly stated your values, or even thought critically about them, there are exercises in chapters 4 and 5 that will help you determine what you value and why it matters. The reason it's important for you to know your values—to deliberately decide what they are—is that they guide the doorkeeper's decisions more deeply than your daily desires and aversions might.

For example, when you look at your current job or even your entire career, what values shaped the decisions you made? If you value financial security, maybe that's because you want to live a physically comfortable life, enjoy unlimited pleasures, or live up to your parents' expectations. Are your parents there in your room telling you that you must have the prestige and security that wealth confers? Or does wealth give you the ability to make charitable contributions or give your children a head start in life? Who influenced those desires?

Even a simple question such as "Why am I in that job?" can lead to a long trail of values and assumptions that might not have been clear until you asked the question. At the core of most of those values and assumptions are the people in your room whose messages you internalized somewhere in your life.

In fact, those messages might have been created by you in reaction to people in your room. Sometimes our strongest unconscious reality is built on the messages we tell ourselves because we want to be accepted, loved, or admired. We create a mindset about ourselves, which is always influenced by who's in the room. (We'll say more about this in chapter 4.)

## The Doorkeeper Decides

What does it mean to let someone into your room? Do you have to include the grocery clerk or the neighbor who walks those yippy little dogs, whom you see every day but with whom you have only the most tenuous relationship?

Going forward, you will learn to think deeply about the rules you set up for admission to your room. You can change the rules when you think it's important; the key to setting up good rules in the first place is to notice what's going on in your room. Here's a simple example: Is that neighbor with the dogs driving you to distraction? Are you making up stories every time they walk by about how people should learn to control their dogs better or that little dogs like that aren't appropriate dogs for the neighborhood or that they should walk their dogs at a more convenient time when you aren't making important work calls from your home office?

If the answer to any of these questions is yes, your door-keeper let them in. The neighbor, the dogs, the anger and frustration you feel—those are all a result of your imaginary doorkeeper letting that sound and story into your room, where you are grasping at the story morning after morning instead of registering the sound of dogs and letting them go scampering down the street without another thought.

By creating rules for what you let into your life, you control the stories you layer onto every event and person in your life. That neighbor might not give you a second thought (it's likely they're not giving you a first thought), but you have them and their pesky dogs right there in your room because you didn't tell the doorkeeper they aren't welcome.

Stewart demonstrates his doorkeeper's simple power with this example: A random person calls him up, asking for his time. It could be someone he sat next to on an airplane, a financial consultant from a national bank soliciting his business, or even someone who has read one of his books. Right then, in that first moment of contact, Stewart asks himself, Do I want to let this person into my room? If the answer is no, he says no. If the person persists, Stewart says, "Look, I might want to let you into my room, but my doorkeeper just won't do it!"

You don't have to put up with drama and intruders in your room if you don't want to. Your doorkeeper works with you to say no and to not give equal weight and attention to everything in your room. But you have to be vigilant. You will need to work with your doorkeeper on a daily basis. (We'll show you how.)

Your doorkeeper has another option: to leave people on the porch. When people want to be in his room, Ivan sometimes imagines they have to stay outside until he knows they can have a real relationship. They're like a salesperson or polltaker arriving at your door and asking for your time. You don't owe them your time and attention. The porch is there for your convenience, not theirs. Ivan uses this image for people with whom he has to interact but who shouldn't have a relationship with him. We all have people like this in our life, neighborhood, and town. Maybe they ride with you in a cycling club or they're a friendly shop owner. Your transactional exchanges with them can be perfectly cordial, but they don't belong in your room.

## The Concierge

Going forward, your doorkeeper will let people into your room or leave them outside on the porch. But once they are in, the doorkeeper returns to the door. Then the question becomes, Where does this person belong?

And what about the people who are already in your room? There's already a crowd of people in there: your significant other, your family members, your friends and work associates, and people you let into your room in the past, either with great consideration or ignorance. A common reaction of people contemplating this reality is "Who let that person in here?" The answer, of course, is you (before you had a doorkeeper)!

Whether they were intentionally let in, accidently allowed in, or just showed up, the people in your room are behaving according to their own rules and values, not yours. Some are off in the distance, and some are right up in your face demanding attention. Many have great love and good intentions for you; some are real trouble. But remember, there's NO EXIT. For good or ill, they are in your room forever.

That's when the concierge becomes the other important person in your room.

The concierge works on your behalf, bringing people closer or walking them farther away. They direct people to their proper place in your room and help make sure everyone stays where they belong. This might be done in a kind, firm, or forceful manner—that's up to you because the concierge is your imaginary ally, entirely under your control and with only your values and interests in mind. (We have friends who call the concierge a bouncer, and if that works for you, go right ahead. But no violence, please.)

Thinking about how your concierge works helps you imagine your room in greater detail. Perhaps your room has many corners or small gathering places or is a vast hall. Everyone belongs somewhere. Some people think of their concierge as a stage manager, making sure everyone is in their proper place. As you contemplate all the places in your room, you can continue to make it grow and give it special places where people go.

Here are some examples of where your concierge might send people:

- *The family place*—Every member of your family, present and past, lives here. They might be as close as siblings or your parents or as distant as a great-grandparent who is influential through the stories told of them. Great-grandfather Labert might be closer to you psychologically than your cousin. If they are in your mind, they are in your room.
- *The workplace*—All the people you currently or previously worked with may dwell here. This means bosses, colleagues, and staff you've supervised. The other auto mechanics at the dealership where you work—they're in there. Mentors, people who have helped you, and customers of all kinds can be guided to the workplace by your concierge.

- *The money place*—This location might be adjacent to the workplace if you see work as mostly a way to get money. It can also include your partner who got you into that good investment or the person who influenced you enough to put your money into a bad investment. People occupy more and less prominent positions in the money place, and that's up to you. Your current business partners and members of your networking group might be near to you, and others far away.
- *The service place*—People who share your interest in serving others gather here. If you belong to a service organization or volunteer for a cause, the people you bring into your life to achieve that work belong here. If you're a churchgoer, this might also be *the faith place*.
- *The childhood place*—Your childhood friends, playmates, teachers, and neighbors exist here. Sometimes you visit this place in memory, where nobody has aged and events that happened decades ago still replay themselves.

Sometimes people occupy only one place (work, church, community, family), and sometimes they wander from one place to another. The concierge is your way to direct them to where they belong or invite them to a different part of your room, perhaps closer than they were to you.

As you and your concierge cooperate to build your desired future, you essentially transform your relationship with the past. Asking, "Who's in my room, and what are they doing here?" helps you mentally and emotionally move people and projects from the foreground to the background. Those troublesome people and events that have had starring roles in the story of your life become mere dots in the distant background. In chapter 6, we'll show you an effective technique for isolating the most undesirable elements that ended up in your room. In this way you create space for who you actually want to be.

## Who Is the "You" in Your Room?
## Barnet's Story

*Barnet Bain is an award-winning movie producer, director, and creativity coach. Select film credits include Oscar winner* What Dreams May Come, *triple Emmy nominee* Homeless to Harvard, The Celestine Prophecy, *and* Milton's Secret.

I was inundated with my own projects and others' requests for my time. I did not know how to say no. Although I work in an industry where saying no is an art form, I must have cut that class at film school.

Many of us are overloaded with opportunities, responsibilities, interests, and obligations, but we can create a doorkeeper within ourselves to police our calendars and commitments (or to take some of the pressure off if we are already overloaded).

My doorkeeper was not some affable Park Avenue doorkeeper in a long overcoat. I enlisted my own personal Seal Team Enforcer, who sees to it that the only people in my room are those I really want there. With my doorkeeper on the case, I quickly began to notice positive changes. Less stress. More energy. A sense of relaxation that comes from being able to choose more and react less.

With new boundaries came new freedoms. For a while I had it made.

Then came my first test.

My wife, Sandi, and I left for our dream vacation. There were supposed to be four segments of travel on both sides of the trip: Los Angeles to Miami, an hour layover, a connecting flight, then the final destination—the warm Caribbean beaches of Saint Martin. As it happened, in three out of the four legs, the aircraft had mechanical problems.

Our first plane sat on the tarmac for more than two hours. Eventually, we landed in Miami, missed our connection, and were forced to stay the night. The next morning there was another airplane and with it another breakdown. We grumbled out of our seats and back to the gate, where we waited—and waited—for a replacement, finally arriving in paradise more than eighteen hours late.

"Stuff happens," I said to Sandi, shrugging it off all Zen-like.

Then the same thing happened five days later. After close to a week of warm breezes and crystalline blue water, I wasn't prepared for another bout of more airport glitches. I could not help noticing the various "me's" that wanted to create a story about the way things were unfolding, the parts of myself that wanted to feel like a victim and find someone to yell at.

I became aware of lots of inner players, like some dysfunctional high school sports team all suited up in my room. There was the me who wanted to blame, the one who craved self-pity, even one who thought he knew how to run an air-line. They were all there with their numbers on, clamoring to get into the game—and the big me, the *me* me, mindful and adult, was frantically trying to manage the team like some beleaguered coach, pleading, "Chill the eff out on the bench!"

That is when I realized, like two sides of a single coin, that a great doorkeeper needed a helper. I added a concierge.

The concierge knows that I have a bunch of players already inside who have been with me all along. When I fall out of the present and into any one of my various pasts, he knows I have been distracted momentarily by parts of myself who are dealing with life from their own developmental levels. With their strong and forceful opinions, they attempt to take over. When their needs are not met or at least acknowledged, a frenzy can ensue—such as me at the airport on the way home from vacation, suntanned and looking relaxed to the untrained eye but seething with agitation inside.

Now the concierge keeps that frenzy from taking over.

Practically speaking, knowing who is showing up at the writers' meeting at Starbucks, at the conference table, at the DMV counter, or at the dinner table helps me manage all my priorities, including the demands on my time and calendar. And as the allies who keep a watchful eye on all my players, both inside and outside my room, my doorkeeper and concierge help me better respond to all of them in ways that alleviate a great deal of upset and angst.

The outcome is that *they* are never running the show.

I am.

## Using Your Doorkeeper and Concierge

The doorkeeper and concierge enable you to start setting parameters for who's in your room and where they are directed. Throughout this book, we share some advice that people have found helpful in this early stage, such as be careful of comparing your insides to other peoples' outsides and don't let people into your room before you have a good idea of whether they belong in there.

Earlier you recognized that you could change how much past mistakes affect you today and in the future. You can relegate them to an out-of-focus section way in the background and move to sharp focus in the foreground the elements of your past that can be building blocks for the future you want.

Some people have asked us if using the doorkeeper and concierge makes you too cold and calculating. If you are constantly weighing whether your relationships are beneficial or detrimental, does life become a long calculation without mystery or surprise? "Are relationships supposed to be only transactional?" they ask. "Is life a game in which I am only looking out after my own interests?"

Not at all! This is a way of making space for mystery and surprise and love and heartbreak and all the other messy, wonderful, human parts of life. An authentic and harmonious life requires deep awareness of what's truly going on in your most important relationships and deliberate choices about where people belong in your room. Socrates's famous observation that "the unexamined life is not worth living" applies to your room—what you do with what you discover is entirely up to you.

## Rules of the Room

There are people who live rent-free in your room. The snide brother-in-law you haven't seen in three years. The nosy neighbor. The politician you've never met but think about daily. The celebrity who obsesses you and will always be richer, better looking, and more famous than you. These people live rent-free in your room. That means they aren't putting anything into the relationship; they never think of you, but somehow they are in there, diverting your attention.

It's not enough to ignore these people if they keep coming back up close to you. You must decide where they belong and then take action. Your concierge can escort some people farther back, into the shadows of the room. Your doorkeeper can be careful not to let others like them through the door.

In the world outside your mind, taking action like this can be as simple as pruning your social media lists to engage with only the people who contribute something of value to your life. They don't all have to be personal friends, but their presence through their work must be positive. As for the others, understand that the stimulation they provide (like righteous anger or secret lust) is keeping you from living your life.

➤ This is a written exercise. Describe the doorkeeper and concierge for yourself. Be as detailed as you can. What do they look like? What clothes do they wear? Do they speak to you or just take directions? They might be real people from your past or imagined people (or if you want to get creative, you can imagine an actor, sports figure, or historical figure, such as a saint or a person you admire—as long as they do their job).

## About Being Nice, Saying No, and the Breaths You Have Left: Geneen's Story

*Geneen Roth is the author of eight books, including the* New York Times *bestsellers* When Food Is Love, The Craggy Hole in My Heart and the Cat Who Fixed It, Women, Food and God, *and* Lost and Found. *She has been teaching groundbreaking workshops and retreats for over thirty years.*

When I was eight, my father gave me a copy of *Death Be Not Proud*, a book by John Gunther about the life and death of his son Johnny. By the time I turned the last page, and I say this in the kindest possible way, I'd become a bit of a hypochondriac and completely death obsessed. I just couldn't believe that an eight-year-old had died—and that everyone else would die as well. It didn't seem fair, and it didn't seem right.

In my twenties and thirties, I elevated my death obsession into a spiritual practice. I learned Buddhist meditation and went to graveyards with teachers who were intent on teaching us what I'd known for years: *Life is short. People die. You will be among them.* I learned so much from my spiritual practice—about ease and loveliness and my crazy mind—but it didn't dispel my fears of death. If anything, it exacerbated them because I became more aware of the shortness of any life. My life, in particular.

But then something unexpected happened. As part of a routine medical procedure, my throat closed, my heart rate skyrocketed, my blood pressure dropped, and I had the strange sensation of leaving my body. I was conscious enough to realize that this was *it*—I was dying. I remember being surprised it was happening so quickly, and on an ordinary day in September. (I was hoping for harps and orchids and long soulful glances of loved ones when I died, not a cold tinny examination room with a nurse wearing a purple happy face pinned to her smock and a doctor with a wandering eye.)

Although there were many compelling insights during (and after) that near-death experience, one that has remained with me is the visceral understanding that all my years of being death obsessed weren't actually about dying or death; they were about life. They weren't about fear of the end, they were about longing to be awake in the middle. I wanted, as the poet Mary Oliver says, to have spent my life "married to amazement," not wedded to regret or exhaustion.

Within a few days of being home from the hospital, I made a list of what I loved. Of what knocked on the door of my heart. Of what I would regret not doing if I had died in that examination room. The list was very short and incredibly simple. It included writing, being with my husband, spending time in nature, working with my students, and being with my friends. It also included not rushing, meeting the eyes of the cashier at the grocery store/gas station/coffee shop, taking time every day to be still, being present with any task, even washing the dishes. I began quitting things I didn't want to participate in. I said no to parties I didn't want to go to, invitations I didn't want to accept. I quit a graduate program in which I was enrolled. I started working on a book I'd wanted to write for years. I spent time with trees, particularly a maple tree in our driveway. I told my husband regularly what I cherished about him and our life together. Over and over, with each day and each choice, I asked myself, Is this something on which I want to spend the breaths I have left? When you realize your breaths are numbered, your choices about what to do with the breaths you have left become radically clear.

Five years have passed, and I am still asking the breath question. Not always, of course. Sometimes when my husband and I are fighting, revenge, not breaths, is uppermost in my mind. But even then, I can often pull myself back from the brink and remember that, really, we are all alive for about ten minutes, and I don't want to miss a moment. Or a breath.

In a complex world—one that rushes at you at times like snowflakes at your windshield—choosing to pay attention to the things you value most is quite a good thing. Another way to look at who and what you let into your room has to do with their costs.

# 3

# Take a Look around Your Room

NOW THAT your doorkeeper and concierge are ready to help, they need to know all about the people in your room. You've already spent a lifetime letting people in, so before anyone else enters, let's consider the people who are there right now. It's time for a more thorough examination of your room.

Take your time—a lot of people are in there with you. We'll help you sort them out, but first, let's get real about what your room is telling you right now. Who is right next to you, and who is far away? Who is getting most of your attention? Maybe your room is extremely loud and full of drama. Conversely, it could be quiet and even a bit boring. Who are the surprising people in your room—the ones you didn't realize were there but are up close and yelling? Why did you let them in?

Consider what you see when we say people are close.

- *Physical proximity*—This might be your family, room-mates, neighbors, or work colleagues. It might be friends you meet at least once a week. Maybe you have a regular dinner with your grown kids and their significant others. See them in your mind's eye being close at hand. Being physically nearby, they can't help but get your attention.

- *Attention-grabbing*—This might be the person who emails or calls you several times a week or the business associate who cc's everyone on every email so you have to open it and decide whether to reply. If you're a frequent user of social media, you might have someone quite close to you because every time you open your timeline, they've posted another picture of their pets or kids or squirrels at their bird feeder. If you think they're not close, why are they getting so much of your attention?

- *Persistent presence*—This might be someone close to you whom you *thought* you had ended a relationship with, such as your first spouse whose voice you somehow still hear or whose good and not-so-good qualities you still recall often.

- *Lingering ghosts*—Close people can even be those in your room who aren't living but still occupy a lot of time in your mind. This is someone with a lot of influence on you, often a parent.

At this early point, you might already have a number of people in mind. It helps to write their names down so you don't waste energy trying to decide exactly where they belong, which will come later.

Some people start these lists on a computer, and that's fine if you prefer to work that way. But if you spend a lot of time at the keyboard for work or at home, we suggest you do this exercise with a paper notebook and pen or pencil. Writing by hand is a more deliberate practice than typing, especially if you slow down by writing in cursive or printing clearly and legibly. You can change the format of pages as you wish. Nobody is going to grade your work—in fact, you don't even have to show it to anyone if you don't want to.

## Who Is Close and Who Is Far Away?

➤ Draw concentric circles with yourself at the center, and decide how close or far away people are today—not where they "should be" but where they are according to the amount of headspace they occupy.

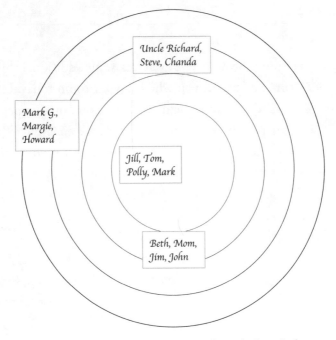

FIGURE 1. One way to map where people are today in the "room" of your mind

Another version of this exercise is to create lists of people according to where they belong or where they came from. Use a column or page for each list, and as you look around your room, place each person on a list. If you like, you can then color-code or give people a number based on how close or far away they are. See an example in table 1.

TABLE 1: Who Is Close and Who Is Far Away?

| Home | Work | Church | Neighborhood |
|------|------|--------|--------------|
| Amy 1 | Jen 3 | Jim R. 2 | Phil 2 |
| Bob 1 | Ashley 3 | Barry C. 3 | Sylvia and Jack 4 |
| Gordon 1 | Tommy 3 | Carolyn C. 3 | Mark and Marie 3 |
| Alice 1 | Scott 3 | Pam S. 4 | Bree 3 |
| Grace 2 | Emma 4 | Beth 2 | Hiro 2 |
| Spencer 2 | | | |

If you get stuck with these exercises, some additional clues in your daily life can tell you who's in your room today. In a notebook, write each of these questions at the top of a page, and then list people who immediately come to mind. The answer to the question can just be a name, and if you want to go a step further toward scoping out your room, you can add a note about the person. As you do, pay attention to your emotional reaction.

Here are the questions:

• Who comes up in my memory often? Is it always the same moment, or do I have many memories that spontaneously seem to come up?

- Whom do I pay instant attention to when they call or write? Why?
- Whom do I resist (e.g., put off answering their calls or emails)?
- Is there someone I resent or have resented for years? Are they close or far?
- Whom do I associate with a recurring stimulus in my life (e.g., the political news)? Do I think of that person more than once a day?
- Whom do I really love or have I loved?
- Do I truly hate someone with enough hatred that just thinking about them can change my mood or have me obsessing about an argument with them?
- Does someone appear often in my dreams? Is it in the same situation or many different ones? Am I still in touch with them today, or do they occupy a purely psychological space in my room?

Here are a couple of sample answers:

- *Whom do I pay attention to when they call or write? Why?*
  I always answer emails from Patricia right away because I know that if I don't, she'll write again the next day, asking me if everything's okay. I guess that means she's pretty close because even though I don't think her emails are important, I don't want to look like I'm ignoring her.
- *Whom do I really love or have I loved?*
  Joanie is the closest person in my room and always will be. Not long after we met, I knew she would be the love

of my life. It's been sixteen years now, and even in hard times I trust and love her completely.

I love my brother. He's had some really tough breaks, but he doesn't complain and just keeps going. I admire his tenacity, and I guess I'd call it courage too. How can I bring him closer?

If you're having trouble creating a list of names, try these techniques:

- List one hundred people from your contacts list or a service like LinkedIn or Facebook. Then group these people according to how much time and energy you invest in each relationship.
- If you don't have a contacts list already, list all the people in your room whose first or last name starts with the letter *A*. Then list all the people in your room whose first or last name starts with the letter *B*. Work your way through the alphabet, and you'll have a list long enough to then sort by each person's proximity to you in your room.

## Rules of the Room

In case you haven't yet realized it, asking "Who's In your room?" is a lifelong process of getting completely honest with yourself. This is not always easy to do because we all have some emotional investment in both the good and bad relationships in our lives. If you find yourself resisting a change in your room, pause and consider what's causing that resistance. In particular, consider whether you've fallen into what investors call the sunk-cost trap: you might be continuing a relationship because of the time you have already invested in it. Since you can't recover that investment, what does that mean for your future?

---

# Expand Your List

The more conscious you are of whom and what you are allowing into your life, the more you can do something about it.

Knowing whom to let in—or not—is crucial because we must live forever with those we let in our rooms. Whoever is in your room *right now* will at least hold a nominal place in it *forever.*

Recent research shows that memories aren't simply forgotten over time. In one study published in the journal *Neuron,* neurobiologist Jeffrey Johnson found that even if study participants couldn't recall specific memories, their brains reacted in a way that showed the memories were still there. Some professionals make intriguing points about the duration and power of memories. Daniel Amen, the psychiatrist and neuroscientist we mentioned earlier, said in an interview for this book, "Memories can't simply be deleted. In fact, the emotions that go with those memories become anchored in your mind."

You can't undo the past, but you *can* curate your room to build a better future. But before the curating process can begin, you need to know whom and what you're dealing with.

When you're comfortable with a high-level list, it's time to take a full inventory. Think about whom you are happy to have in your room and whom you'd like to evict if you could.

This process is personal, but we encourage you to think through this list of categories of people as you assess your life. This is truly just a starting place to give you inspiration. Consider how many people are on this list and in your room. Don't just skim the list; think about the many people in your room who fit into each category below and write their names.

- Family members
- Friends and acquaintances
- Neighbors and community members
- Business associates (e.g., partners, clients, vendors) and colleagues
- Members of organizations or groups you are a member of (spiritual, social, business, sports, etc.)
- Social media contacts, especially those you engage with, reply to, message, or retweet
- Other "screen time" contacts, such as people you watch on television (e.g., news) or follow (e.g., bloggers)—if they are in your head, you're allowing them in your room
- People to whom you have made commitments, such as members of a school committee or fundraising event

You can see how crowded your room is when you consider everyone. Some people shudder as they think of whom they have let in their rooms. Others are fairly pleased with their list but then scratch their heads when they begin to wonder why in the world they accepted social media friend requests from people who bullied them in high school.

When you have an inventory of the people in your room, you can start assessing the resonance each person brings to your room and your life. In the next chapter, we'll show you how to work with the most influential people there.

## Two Daily Visualizations

➡ In chapter 1, you visualized your room in detail. That was a project. This exercise is a short practice, one that you can do briefly twice a day. Have your notebook nearby; new ideas about your room might occur to you at any time.

*Morning*—See your room in detail. Who is nearby, and who is far away? Who is indistinct, and who is close? Why?

*Evening*—Who was near during the day? Who was far? How did you interact and why? Were they there for good or ill?

Similar to the daily review in many spiritual practices, this short practice helps you clarify what's going on in your room and decide what you will do about it.

---

### Money and You: Matt's Story

*Matt Weinstein, the founding president of a California innovative team-building consulting company, travels internationally, is an award-winning speaker, and had a PBS special called Fun Works!*

I was on vacation in Antarctica with my former college roommates. I know, it's no kind of beach! But we had a spectacular voyage on a Russian icebreaker and saw penguins everywhere while gorgeous icebergs floated all around us like spectacular works of sculpture, and breathtaking scenery came into view everywhere we looked.

About halfway through the voyage, I was paged over the loudspeaker to go to the bridge for a satellite phone call. I went dashing up the stairs to the bridge to get my phone call because I knew these satellite calls cost ten dollars a minute. When I picked up the phone, it was my wife, Geneen. Her voice was calm and steady, but her first few words turned my life upside down: "Bernie Madoff has been arrested. His entire fund is a complete scam."

We had just lost our entire life savings.

We didn't even know if we would be able pay the mortgage anymore. We talked anxiously on the phone for a few more minutes until one of us (her, I believe) had the presence of mind to say to the other, "You know what, Sweetheart, we are no longer the kind of people who can afford to talk on a satellite telephone at ten dollars a minute!" so we hung up.

Geneen and I were finally reunited ten days later. We decided that although Madoff had stolen our money, he wouldn't steal the rest of our lives as well. As the philosopher Joseph Campbell so beautifully put it, sometimes "we must be willing to let go of the life we have planned so as to have the life that is waiting for us."

I got back to work as soon as I could. I needed to work as much as possible to start earning some money. For the past forty years, I've been teaching people about building community through laughter, play, and fun. But in order to authentically talk about the power of laughter and play, I had to get back in touch with the possibility of laughter and play in my own life in spite of the disastrous circumstances. Geneen went back to completing her latest book, *Women, Food and God*. Both of us were on fire with creative projects. Although our finances were decimated, we had come to peace with it and were moving on and happy in our work and full of aliveness and excitement.

Oprah Winfrey read *Women, Food and God* and loved it and wrote about it in *O, The Oprah Magazine*. She devoted two complete shows on the Oprah Winfrey Network to the book. As a result, *Women, Food and God* was a huge number one *New York Times* bestseller. Nearly as quickly as we had lost all our money, it all came back.

As one of our close friends said to us at the time, "Well, you weren't poor for very long!"

In fact, it had happened before. Years ago, I was ripped off by my long-term financial advisor. A close friend heard the news and said, "I feel so bad about what happened to you. I know an exclusive fund that hasn't lost money in thirty years of existence. I can get you in." That fund was—you guessed it—Madoff Investment Securities.

After that second loss, I realized that for a long time I had been placing my money with father substitutes—people who would take care of me with respect to money so I wouldn't have to take responsibility for my own decisions. That way I could feel special and protected, and I wouldn't have to educate myself on the difficult realities of money management. That's who was in my room.

This time around I learned some basic rules of financial management, like not to invest in anything I don't understand and to diversify, diversify, diversify. And, yes, I have taught my doorkeeper to keep the father figures who still look appealing out of my room. More importantly, I've learned that the one trustworthy person to let into my room when it comes to financial matters is the grown-up version of myself—a version who has learned some essential financial lessons the hard way and is able to educate himself about money matters and take responsibility for his actions. Though, of course, Oprah can drop by anytime she wants.

You might think of your room as something that can fly on automatic pilot once you have the template in place. But, remember, you're the one who configures that automatic pilot. You have to learn to trust yourself when setting the controls, and you have to remember to stay in the room yourself.

# 4

# Dealmakers and Dealbreakers

CLEARING FRENZY and chaos from your life with a room, a doorkeeper, and a concierge can be quite calming. But they need training to do their jobs. How do they know whom to let in and where to lead them? We have observed people struggling with this question from every angle and found that the most effective way to train the doorkeeper and concierge is to make them ultrasensitive to peoples' values. Values are the foundation of all the relationships in your room, the decision framework for letting people in, and the standards by which you decide where they belong. Values are the vote. That means becoming clear on your values and creating a personal declaration of purpose concerning whom you will let into your room in the future and why.

First, you need to understand that *what consumes your time controls your mind.* That goes for work, play, and the people you spend time with. What is consuming your time these days, and how do you feel about that? If you're not happy about what's consuming your time, there's good news: you can change that. This change begins with the values you manifest.

We cannot name your most important values. We also can't help you work on who's in your room until you have a better sense of the values you'll use to make decisions about who belongs there. If you do this, you'll begin to see changes in how you think about the people in your life, which will then lead to positive changes in all of your life.

You can take as much or as little time as you want, but we hope you will consider the significance of this exercise. If you want to control your room and your life, you need to work through your values. Knowing your values in detail is the basis for curating the room you desire. And it won't hurt, we promise.

People talk a lot about their values, but we're going to side with the simple rule that values are expressed more in deed than word. Jerry Porras, Lane Professor Emeritus of Organizational Behavior and Change at the Stanford University Graduate School of Business, told us, "I don't believe in words anymore; I only believe in behaviors." We agree.

In this chapter, you'll make the connection between the values that matter to you and the people in your room who do or don't share those values through their actions. Value-naming is a big project; for our purpose, we'll limit it to your listing and deeply understanding which values are most important to you.

When we speak to large audiences, we always ask, "Can you name your values, the handful of concepts, beliefs, or aspirations in your life that you deem most important?"

The silence can be deafening when we ask that question.

# Identify Your Dealbreakers

Rarely can people list their top values when asked without advance notice. With so many to choose from, how can you prioritize them?

Here's one shortcut that always works: list your dealbreakers. People struggle to make a complete list of values, but they know their dealbreakers. For example, that person in your life who is all take and no give, who drains you emotionally—they're a dealbreaker. They're still in your room (you let them in long ago), but they don't have to be close. This step is an important part of assessing your values. Everyone needs to have a dealbreaker list, your "don't even think about it" list. It includes values, behaviors, attributes, characteristics, projects, and so on, that you just won't tolerate—period.

Dealbreakers are like a flashlight that illuminates your values when that word seems abstract, identifying what you *won't* let into your life. Plus, explaining why can lead you to the early training of your doorkeeper and concierge. The process will also lead you toward understanding what you *will* let in.

Every time we ask whether someone knows a dealbreaker, they come up with at least a few. Maybe they're so memorable because they make such a strong negative impression!

The traits you most deplore in others are good dealbreakers to list, such as laziness, duplicity, lying, being late, power-tripping, interrupting, breaking commitments, inauthenticity, greed, selfishness—we could go on forever. Think of someone who exhibits one of those traits, someone who makes you angry or your skin crawl. Ask yourself what specific behavior gets under your skin, and then ask what its opposite is—that opposite is probably a value you care about.

Let your imagination run free with this thought experiment. You probably don't have a shortage of examples. If you want to make a long list, go ahead. Later you can distill your biggest dealbreakers down to a choice few.

Doug knows a person who tipped him off to a value he hadn't considered much. This person is an internationally known expert in a difficult field, with decades of brilliant success. They are also considerate, loving, and even sentimental. But they interrupt conversations constantly. They finish his sentences (and everyone else's). They push their opinion into every discussion.

You could call that person rude or inconsiderate and say that the logical opposite of that is consideration or politeness. Write that down. Then look a little deeper into the behavior, and you could say the person is bossy (opposite values: courtesy and empathy). You might say they don't listen (opposite values: curiosity and kindness). You could even say this person grates so much on the nerves because they don't acknowledge the potential contributions of others and are selfish (opposite values: considerate and selfless).

Do you see where this leads? The people in your room who drive you crazy can reveal some of your most treasured values by holding a mirror up to them. They are dealbreakers because you don't want to be in a relationship with someone who violates your values.

Get your notebook and make that first list of dealbreakers. Take time with this exercise. It might help to reflect on the following questions:

- When was the last time you were really angry and frustrated? Why?
- What makes your life less fulfilling than you think it should be?
- What is it that you most dislike about certain behaviors?
- What do you regard as the lowest depth of misery?
- What do you find troubling about your friends?

After you have thought about the questions, write down your list of dealbreakers. This list can be constructed from your responses to the questions above and from another source: simply record behaviors you despise. Write down the behaviors or traits that, when you observe them, seem like nails running across a chalkboard. These dislikes could be things like lying, creating drama, grossly exaggerating, being irresponsible, acting stubborn, or one-upping. In other words, take a moment to list behaviors you can't stand.

Two cautionary notes as you write the names (or maybe just the initials in case you want to keep it confidential for now): First, there are going to be dealbreakers who, one way or another, are in a relationship with you. We'll talk about them later. For now, it's important to consider what qualities the dealbreakers exhibit.

Second—and this is a tough one—dealbreakers sometimes hold up an uncomfortable mirror to your own behaviors. That person who interrupts all the time made Doug consider how often he interrupted or dismissed people unconsciously, usually because his mind was racing ahead to the next idea. He had to consciously learn to listen better because knowing he valued empathy, kindness, growth, and selflessness, he had to change his behavior to align with his values. He had learned about Carol Dweck's growth mindset and determined he could learn to overcome that shortcoming, which was tipped off by that irritating person in his room.

Next, create a set of rules or attributes that will help you make better decisions in your life. We've created some examples to get the creativity flowing. You need to determine your own rules for people you want to let into your room and for your dealbreakers.

Here are examples of how you can describe dealbreakers for the people you *won't* let into your room from this point forward:

- I will not tolerate anyone who is controlling or narcissistic.
- I will not tolerate anyone who is always late and forgetful.
- I will not tolerate anyone who complains all the time and acts needy.
- I will not tolerate anyone who introduces excess drama into my life.

As with the other exercises, time is your friend. You might start with long, disjointed lists. But if you revisit them, you'll likely be able to boil down your dealbreakers to just a handful of concepts. Or you might list a couple of people. That's fine because the next exercise is a lot more pleasant.

---

## Rules of the Room

Addition by subtraction.

Ivan tells people who run BNI chapters that sometimes if you want a chapter to grow, you have to cut members loose. It's like pruning rosebushes—addition by subtraction.

Even if you can't get someone out of your room, you can keep their baggage out. That means putting boundaries on their behavior, refusing to engage, walling them off, or directing your concierge to take them to a far corner of your room. When you subtract other people's bad behavior from your life, you are actually adding to your life.

---

## Identify Your Dealmakers

Next, start a list of your dealmakers. These are the people you will let into your room from this point forward. This list will help you consider whether you allow a relationship of any kind to begin based on someone's values as shown in the things they do (and to a lesser extent, the things they say).

This exercise is the opposite of the dealbreakers exercise. That one came first because we've seen how it resonates instantly with people. This one can be a bit harder to pin down because we can take for granted what makes our dealmakers special. If we pick the closest people—those we love or treasure—it can be tricky to isolate their values from their other beautiful qualities. It might be better to start with someone who isn't a partner or family member, and ask, Whom do I admire?

What traits do you admire in people you know and like? They might be courage, integrity, gentleness, perseverance, loyalty, knowledge, or spontaneity. Think of someone you know who exhibits those traits, someone who is already in your room because you like being around them.

We know someone who built a successful business while working as a consultant to large corporations regarding their compensation practices. He is always upbeat and positive and gives huge amounts of time to his community. Nobody who didn't know his life story would suspect that he lost his mother at an early age, lost his closest sibling to suicide, was divorced, and endured other tragedies that would turn many people angry, bitter, and self-pitying. Yet this person has somehow transformed his personal losses into inexhaustible compassion and kindness toward others. He's a dealmaker on our list for those qualities.

If you find yourself second-guessing a quality that you came up with, thinking it's not a value, ask why it appeals to you. That will point to a value. For example, maybe you wrote down a name and put beside it "funny" or "witty." Are those values? Not exactly—they're skills or personality traits—but they point to something you enjoy in others, such as friendliness in a person who is always making people laugh or wisdom in someone whose wit is based on life experience. You value that trait.

One emotional cue that works for some people comes from asking yourself, Is there someone you both like *and* envy a little based on values they exhibit? Envy can work like the positive version of someone holding a mirror to our values. Don't focus on your envy of possessions or wealth; think instead of someone about whom you say, "I'd love to be as generous as she is because generosity means so much to me." The point is not to become exactly like that person but, again, to identify the values that mean the most to you.

Stewart is friends with Brooke McDonnell and Helen Russell, founders of Equator Coffees. He could just say, "They're lovely people," but that doesn't go deep enough. Looking at their story, it's clear they display wonderful values. Brooke and Helen are *committed* to making people's lives better through coffee, and they walk the talk when it comes to farmers, roasters, workers, and supporters. Equator Coffees is B Corp certified, which means it has passed a rigorous set of standards that prove it balances purpose and profit to the benefit of all. Brooke and Helen have *persevered* in their vision for more than twenty-five years. They have insanely *high-quality* standards, and, when it comes to business, everything they do is aligned with their beliefs, which is the definition of *integrity*.

From thinking about these two friends, Stewart includes on his list commitment, perseverance, quality standards, and integrity. He admires these values, so they go on the list. In 2016 Equator Coffees was the first LGBTQ-owned business to be named National Small Business of the Year by the Small Business Administration, so success and accomplishment go on the list as well.

Just like the last exercise (but more fun), create a set of rules or attributes that will help you make better decisions in your life. The people with those values are your first set of dealmakers.

Here are some examples of rules for the people you *will* let into your room from this point forward:

- They must contribute an equal amount to the relationship.
- They must work in a field that has a positive impact in the world.
- They must be loyal and honest.
- They must be open-minded and have a sense of humor.

By now you have named a few dealbreakers and the values they transgress as well as some dealmakers who exhibit the values you believe in. It's time to work from the inside out now and make a longer list of your most important values.

## Listing Your Own Values

In teaching the importance of values, we've frequently witnessed the personal revelations people have had once they take the time to sit down and actually think about their values. Creating your list of values can be as straightforward or as layered a process as you'd like. The goal—however you achieve it—is for you to recognize, acknowledge, and establish a defined set of objectives and explicit values by which you live. These values will allow you to make decisions about who gets past your doorkeeper and enters your room.

Your values can be current, or they can be aspirational. Your aspirational values are ones that you desire to achieve in life. To this end, we ask that, for maximum benefit, you recognize the values you *do* act on and live by and which ones you are *striving* for. Doing so will give you clarity as we teach you how to manage who's in your room later in the book. For the purposes of this exercise, aspirational values are important but different. Your current values are the ones you act on, and your aspirational values are the ones you are striving for.

➡️ Below is a starter list of possible values that might resonate with you. Values can be written as words, groups of words, or complete sentences, as we'll show you later in this chapter. The list below is simply to get you to start thinking about what your values may be. Feel free to mark the ones that resonate with you and add any others that apply to you.

*Achievement*—Accomplishing what you set out to do

*Adventure*—Undertaking exciting and unfamiliar experiences

*Authenticity*—Behaving according to your values and beliefs

*Belonging*—Feeling connected to and liked by others

*Commitment*—Directing yourself wholeheartedly to a goal or promise

*Community*—Feeling a meaningful connection to a group of people

*Compassion*—Feeling sympathy, care, or concern for others

*Competence*—Being effective at what you do

*Conscientiousness*—Acting in a principled and thorough manner

*Courage*—Standing up for your beliefs

*Drive*—Directing energy and focus toward a goal until it's achieved

*Empathy*—Understanding how others feel

*Endurance*—Sustaining effort toward a goal despite difficulties and/or setbacks

*Equality*—Respecting everyone's right to parity

*Family*—Taking care of and spending time with loved ones

*Financial security*—Increasing your wealth so you have as much as you need

*Forgiveness*—Granting pardon or absolving someone else of a wrong

*Freedom*—Embracing liberty and exercising choice and free will

*Friendship*—Experiencing close ongoing relationships

*Giving*—Extending your time, money, and talents to a cause or person

*Gratitude*—Appreciating kindness or beneficial acts

*Growth*—Advancing toward greater skill, belief, maturity, and goals

*Health*—Improving your physical and psychological well-being

*Helping*—Taking care of others and meeting their needs

*Humility*—Seeing your true significance in relation to all

*Independence*—Controlling your own thoughts and circumstances

*Innovation*—Finding new and creative ways of doing things

*Integrity*—Aligning your actions with your beliefs

*Justice*—Pursuing what is fair and morally right

*Knowledge*—Acquiring intellectual stimulation and new ideas

*Leadership*—Guiding people and projects and setting the pace

*Lifelong learning*—Embracing continuous curiosity and mental and emotional growth

*Loyalty*—Being faithful to your word, commitments, and loved ones

*Making a difference*—Having a positive impact in accordance with your values

*Mentoring*—Leading and guiding another by sharing wisdom, skills, and experience

*Obligation*—Feeling a sense of duty or responsibility

*Opportunity*—Having the chance to experience progress and advancement

*Partnership*—Joining forces with others in a common effort

*Perseverance*—Continuing toward a goal despite setbacks or difficulties

*Personal growth*—Pursuing new skills and self-awareness

*Pleasure*—Seeking personal enjoyment and fun

*Power*—Having the ability to influence others

*Recognition*—Getting noticed for your efforts

*Relationships*—Putting effort into valued connections with others

*Responsibility*—Keeping your word and being accountable

*Risk*—Exploring the unknown and testing the limits

*Security*—Being free from danger or threat

*Service*—Devoting time and gifts to a greater purpose or cause

*Spiritual growth*—Seeking connection to a higher purpose

*Spontaneity*—Acting without reservation in the moment

*Success*—Accomplishing goals of all kinds

*Synergy*—Joining with others whose gifts differ to achieve new goals

*Teamwork*—Acting with others according to agreed norms and frameworks

*Tolerance*—Being open to different ideas

*Tradition*—Respecting an established way things have been done

*Travel*—Experiencing new places in the world in every way

*Wisdom*—Applying knowledge, judgment, and beliefs to particular circumstances

We've offered some simple definitions, but you can define any value in a way that feels right to you. You are seeking a body-and-soul, heart-and-mind resonance here. There are no right answers except those with which you feel authentically connected. You don't need to complete this in one sitting, and you are definitely not in competition with anyone. Give yourself the space to live with your responses and make revisions as your values get progressively clearer to you. It goes without saying—but we'll say it anyway—you must be relentlessly honest.

People often benefit from using a process of elimination when identifying their top values. To do this, circle the ten values on this partial list that resonate the most for you and then slowly eliminate three or four of them in order to get to your more important values.

To verify your answers, think about how you would be acting if a selected word or phrase represented a core value of yours. Sentence completion can help immensely. Start off the sentence with "If this truly mattered to me, I would . . ." and go wherever it leads you. Your final list likely will encompass terms that you actively live by and also strongly reflect the person you aspire to become.

Here are a few examples of this sentence-completion exercise to get you thinking:

- If *financial security* truly mattered to me, I would stop running up credit card debt on stuff I don't need and instead start fully contributing to my savings or retirement plan each year.
- If *service* and *making a difference* truly mattered to me, I would stop talking about volunteering and instead choose a charity to volunteer with each week.
- If *responsibility* truly mattered to me, I would stop blaming others for my failures.

The above exercise might not be easy, but remember that you can't live your values if you don't acknowledge where you're falling short.

---

## Rules of the Room

Goals and values go hand in hand. The power of using these with your own doorkeeper over the course of your lifetime can lead to huge positive differences in how your life turns out. Only when you are living your values and surrounding yourself with like-minded people can you become clear on your life's purpose while also gaining clarity on your objectives.

As you bring people and projects into your life that fully align with your purpose, your values, and your objectives, those positive decisions will compound over time, and your life will gain momentum. But beware because the opposite is true as well. If you pay no attention to the types of people and stuff that you allow into your life and you operate in a random fashion—the way most people do—then your life will become chaotic and unmanageable.

---

Sometimes people have a difficult time being honest about what they truly value right now and what they would like to value in the future (i.e., their aspirational values). The reality is, your current values are where you are investing your time now, and your aspirational values (i.e., the values you would *like* to exhibit in your life) are what you want to manifest in your life. If we were to follow you around with a video camera for a week, we would quickly learn what you truly value by what you actually prioritize in your life right now. If we could somehow do that, how often would we record you doing things completely out of alignment with your declared values?

Do you value patience but honk at slow drivers? Do you value consideration but habitually arrive late to meetings? Is spiritual growth important to you but you keep saying, "I'll get to that someday," rather than reading spiritual texts or meditating for fifteen minutes a day?

These little disconnects between what you value and what you do are signposts directing you to live in a way that is more aligned with your true beliefs. They aren't all dramatic sins; they are unproductive behaviors that found their way into your life—into the room of your life—usually by small incremental steps or compromises. Now is the time to take all the unproductive behaviors and values and replace them with new values that will create a more fulfilling life for you.

If you wish to do a comprehensive online values assessment, Tony Alessandra, a good friend of ours, has developed an online platform called Assessments 24x7 that will help you start to get a good picture of the values (or what he calls *motivators*) that are important to you.

The Motivators assessment identifies seven potential drivers of one's values, or motivation, which exist in everyone to varying levels. By taking detailed measurements of these seven key impulses, the Motivators assessment is able to offer the practical applications and insight necessary to maximize performance and project outcomes. You can get one of these comprehensive reports by visiting the Motivators page on Assessments24x7 .com.

## Are You Still Struggling?

It can be tempting to write down what you *think* your values should be, while being somewhat hazy about what they actually *are*. If this happens, it will create conflict for you down the road. An excellent way to avoid this trap is to think of the five people you most like spending time with—your best dealmakers. Take five sheets of paper and put one name on the top of each sheet. Next, select seven to ten values that best describe each of your friends' core values. Review the five sheets and look for the most commonly identified values and write them down, up to ten values. It's a good bet these are your own core values because you resonate with them in your friends.

If the list does not reflect who you want to be or become, then it's time to get busy. You are going to need a new circle of friends in your room—people who live in alignment with your values and what matters to you. Your life is a reflection of the five or six people that you spend the most time with (remember: *you become whom you're with*). If your core group of friends is composed of solid, hard-working, fulfilled people who rarely complain, odds are that you are this way too; however, if your core group of friends are toxic people who drink heavily and have many broken relationships, then this is likely present in your life too.

## Some Lessons Cost More Than Others: Ivan's Story Part I

*Ivan tells a story about how any person in your room has the potential to teach you and why you must pay attention.*

A few years ago my company was in the midst of one of the largest projects in the history of our organization. The project involved many people and was incredibly complex and financially challenging. It was also in trouble. I needed to select a key player for the project team. The man I chose had incredibly strong technical skills. He was highly qualified for the project and was the perfect person to help turn this around—or so I thought. I knew, however, he came with a lot of baggage. He didn't always play well with others. From time to time he would fly off the handle emotionally when talking to people, bringing an immense amount of drama to the workplace.

I have lived most of my life as a highly rational guy. I can relate to Spock from *Star Trek*, though I don't have the pointed ears. Although my gut was sending out yellow alerts, I hired him. I suspected there would be problems with the drama and the outbursts—however, I believed I could coach and guide him through this.

It turns out I was wrong. Monumentally wrong. Despite his incredible technical skills, his behavior more than offset his technical strengths. The project went from problematic to horrific within a year. It was way over budget, well behind schedule, and not nearly of the quality that I expected. Because he didn't share information freely, most of the people in the project didn't understand or know many of its aspects.

It wasn't so bad that I would come into meetings and get immediately derailed by a shouting match. He wasn't given to leaping about the room in business attire, shouting, throwing things, knocking over chairs like Bobby Knight on steroids. When you see that type of behavior, you suspect the person has a serious disorder.

It wasn't as obvious or deliberate as that. At first, it seemed just a case of bad chemistry, of not getting along or being a team player. Keep in mind that I really needed this person and had made a logical decision to put up with almost anything to get the project done. Well, I was wrong, as I said, but it took me a while to admit just how wrong. I'd gotten by with worse, I told myself. But maybe I hadn't. Maybe this was my new worst.

When I first came across the notion of "Who's in your room?" I decided right then and there that this project leader should never have been in my room.

I understood that removing him from the project was going to be difficult and painful. But I was clear on the reality that it had to be done. It ended up taking months to lay the groundwork with everyone on the team, with me personally engaging them in pieces of the project they needed to know but weren't privy to because of this manager's dysfunctional control needs. I had to drop many of my normal responsibilities and devote an immense amount of time to this process. I promoted some people and moved others around. When all was ready, I made the move and let go of the project leader. There was an immediate and palpable change in the project. Today it is becoming exactly the product that I was hoping for, and I am proud of it as an entrepreneur.

The lesson I learned in this very expensive and very stressful process was this: don't allow people in just because of their technical skills. I want a work environment that is a drama-free zone, and I now pick people for my organization who I want in my room. I now try to select qualified people who fit an organizational culture of collaboration, people who share information and knowledge and don't bring to the process an Emmy Award–winning soap opera of behaviors.

I also learned another lesson. I need to trust my gut. I hear that's called *head-heart balance*. My doorkeeper and I are working on it.

# Linking Your Values
# to Your Life

AN HONEST assessment of whether you actually *live* your values today prepares you to identify where your values and behavior are in conflict. The key to a healthy room is linking your values to your life—in other words, living authentically.

When you have written a good long list of values (it doesn't have to be final), write a sentence or two after each describing how this value is important to you and how you express it through your behavior. It's helpful to think of the different areas of your life where your values come into play. For each value, you might write a sentence or two, or you can sort the descriptions according to how that value is part of a list of life categories, such as professional values, parenting values, social life values, family values, and values on where to invest money.

Here is a sample list of personal values and descriptions:

- *Family*—My family is my personal foundation. I cherish my time with my spouse and family, and I look for opportunities to grow with them.

- *Relationships and teamwork*—I seek opportunities to grow and nurture strong, loving relationships with quality individuals, and I know I will be more successful when I foster teamwork.
- *Leadership/mentoring/coaching*—I believe leadership is one of the most important attributes of my success. I seek like-minded mentors, colleagues, and employees. I enjoy both opportunities to mentor and coach others as well as being mentored and coached myself.
- *Physical and spiritual well-being*—I maintain healthy practices, including diet, exercise, and meditation, and I avoid things that may damage my health or psyche.
- *Lifelong learning*—I believe that learning doesn't end with school. Learning is something I want to be engaged in throughout my entire life.

## Today's To-Dos

Look at your list of today's to-dos. For each item, ask if it involves someone in your room and where they belong. Say aloud a value of yours that this to-do item will fulfill. If it's something really simple, such as "Call to confirm a hair appointment," you can say, "Looking my best is good. I have a light, chatty relationship with this hairdresser, so they're in my room but not up close." If an item is more involved, such as a work meeting, consider the people you'll be working with, the relationship you have with each, and how close they might be. You might discover your concierge has some work to do rearranging your room. And if not, you can take a moment to appreciate the good place your room is becoming.

# Values Make the Difference: Stephanie's Story

*Our friend and collaborator Rick Sapio told us this story about sharing his perspective on values with his good friend Stephanie.*

Several years ago, Stephanie came to me about a family emergency. She was at the end of her rope. You see, she had four daughters, and Bonnie, the oldest one, who was eighteen years old at the time, had been in a deep, passionate, and turbulent relationship with a twenty-year-old drug dealer. This relationship had gone on for more than two years, and it was wreaking havoc on Stephanie's peace of mind and, more importantly, on her three younger daughters.

Bonnie would go days without coming home and would occasionally rob her family of money and jewelry. Stephanie tried every conceivable option to save her daughter and her family. But the behavior continued.

I suggested to Stephanie that she teach her daughter values-based decision-making and the doorkeeper and concierge principles. One morning, Stephanie sat down with her daughter and framed out a list of values and what they meant. They talked about integrity, motherhood, health, honor, and relationships. They made a list of Bonnie's most treasured values.

Stephanie then asked her daughter to imagine allowing a doorkeeper to stand at the entrance to the room of her life. She asked her daughter to next imagine that this doorkeeper had the power to *not* let anyone or anything into the room of her life if it did not align with her newly stated values. She explained that Bonnie's concierge could guide people who damaged her values to a kind of isolation ward for the people who are in your room but are no good for you [a place we'll describe in the next chapter].

The entire meeting between Stephanie and her daughter took about thirty minutes.

Stephanie called me a couple of months later in tears. That morning, Bonnie came down to breakfast as usual, but something seemed different about her. She seemed calmer than she had been during all the turmoil of the preceding months. Stephanie and her husband quietly sat there in shock as their daughter explained to them that she had broken up with her boyfriend and that she would never see him again.

When the parents asked why, their daughter said, "Simple: he really didn't align with my values."

How much future destruction, drug use, jail time, and other damage did this simple little thirty-minute exercise save Stephanie and her family? You may or may not have a situation this serious in your life, but how much will your future be impacted by applying the lessons in this book to your life?

We'd like you to imagine drawing a line in the sand of your life right now. From this point forward, imagine that every future decision you make regarding who or what gets into the room of your life is completely and wholly aligned with your newly stated values. Now imagine what your life will be like if you compound these powerful decisions one on top of the other for the rest of your life.

# Your Values and the People in Your Room

This exercise is a deeper dive into the work you started when you thought about your five friends in the last chapter. Go back to the inventory of the people in your room you made in chapter 3, and note which ones truly share your values. You can return to this activity many times—the longer you take, the more fully you will understand which values are most important and how people demonstrate those values by their behavior. It's most helpful to ask *who* questions.

➡ Here are some to get you thinking:

- Who brings in things that align with your values?
- Who brings you joy?
- Who offers you support?
- Who is happy for you when something good happens?
- Who accepts you just as you are?
- Whom do you learn from and view as a teacher or mentor?
- Who brings out the best in you?
- Who makes you feel most alive when you are with them?

After thinking through those questions, write a sentence or two that explains why you value the person and then link those sentences to your values. If you want to frame it in the past tense, that's okay. After all, once someone is introduced into our lives, their memory is anchored in our mind forever. Write reasons why you have good associations with people in your room. Here are some potential examples of what we mean:

*Family*—My parents love and support me unconditionally, and they have done so when I was a child and as an adult. They are always there for me, as I am for them, even if we don't always agree. (Values = family, close relationships)

*Spouse*—My spouse is my partner in life. They have been there with me through thick and thin, and we can always count on each other for a good laugh, a warm hug, or a shoulder to cry on. (Values = commitment, close relationships)

*Friends*—My running buddy keeps me motivated and accountable to reach my fitness goals. (Values = fitness, friendship)

*Community members*—My neighbors are good people who are there to lend a hand, and I find joy in helping them when they need it too. (Values = community, friendship)

*Work associates*—My business colleagues are trusted friends whom I support and also learn from. (Values = friendship, learning, adding value)

Next, ask yourself the opposite: who brings in things that don't align with my values? Make a list of people who cause you the most pain and grief because they don't align with your stated values. These people are holding you back, and you must learn how to deal with them. (We'll have more for you about this later.)

Remember—it's far more onerous to deal with someone once they're in your life than it is not to allow that person into your life in the first place. Think of a time in your life when you've chosen what you believe represents a good opportunity but have brought people into your room who don't represent your values. You'll begin to notice how this opportunity has probably cost you time, energy, or money—and likely all three.

In contrast to the list above, identify relationships with some people on your list that clash with your values, such as in the following examples:

> *Friendship with [name of person]*—This friendship drains me because my friend calls only to complain or ask for a big favor. They will never listen to advice from me or anyone else. This violates my dealbreaker rule of not having anyone in my room who introduces drama into my life. Also, our phone calls take time away from family, which is one of my values.

> *Board membership*—I thought I wanted to be on this charity's board of directors, but the board's disorganization is driving me insane, and we aren't accomplishing anything. Although I joined the board to add value, I'm unable to accomplish that goal; the resistance to change is much stronger than my will to fight for something that is taking time away from my personal life.

> *Three-quarters of my social media friends*—Rather than getting enjoyment from social media, I get frustrated because much of what I see posted from my contacts does not align with my values. Rather than feeling connected with the distant friends and family I am deeply committed to, I feel disheartened.

# Write a Personal Declaration

Many people benefit from writing a personal declaration, which offers another angle to gain insights about you and who's in your room.

A personal declaration helps you consider how your values add to the most important goals and beliefs in your life. It contains sections that break down your values into different categories of your life. You can categorize your life in many ways, but we like to use these seven: (1) business/career, (2) financial, (3) family, (4) health and well-being, (5) spiritual, (6) friends and social life, and (7) fun (i.e., where do you want to have fun in your life?). The document points toward your "purpose" in life, what your most important values are, what your formula for success has been, what your legacy will be, what your long-term intentions are in those seven areas, what your goals are given those intentions, and any affirmations or motivational and inspirational quotes that you like. We've filled in this form with the possible answers from a forty-five-year-old owner of a tech services company.

Purpose:
My life's purpose is to spread joy in all my endeavors, through business, family, and community life.

My formula for success in life:
I have always loved to take charge and lead people.

One word that describes my work:
Efficiency.

What I would like my legacy to be:
My legacy is the many people I have taught to operate their businesses efficiently. My advice is still relevant and used after I'm gone.

My most important values: (Fill in one to five values or goals for each category below.)

*Business/career*—efficiency, integrity, success, joy, legacy

*Financial/material*—independence, house, kids' education, travel

*Family*—health for all, lifelong romance, grandchildren

*Health/well-being*—continue running, less anxiety, moderation

*Spiritual*—church community, lifelong spiritual growth, learning, time in nature

*Social*—extended family, recognition of my accomplishments, active member of my service organization

*Fun*—time with spouse and kids, travel, golf, classic movies

My long-term intentions:

*Business/career*—I am running a tech services company with $7 million or more in revenue.

*Financial*—Our household net worth is over $2 million by age sixty.

*Family*—My family is healthy, close, and growing.

*Health/well-being*—My health is better than that of 80 percent of my peers.

*Spiritual*—My spiritual life is always growing, based on regular church attendance, meditation, and study.

*Social*—My community is healthy, welcoming, and full of active people.

*Fun*—I regularly enjoy running, playing golf, watching classic movies, and spending time with family.

My goals: (List as many goals as you'd like for each category below. They can be small or large, as long as they are aligned with your intentions.)

*Business/career*—Become a "best small business to work at" within five years.

*Financial*—Maximize retirement savings.

*Family*—Go on two family vacations every year, with no work interruptions.

*Health/well-being*—Maintain my ideal weight; attend one retreat every year.

*Spiritual*—Participate in a four-day spiritual retreat this year.

*Social*—Host six to eight dinner parties this year, inviting different guests.

*Fun*—Run a marathon time under four and a half hours; have a golf handicap of eleven.

My favorite motivational quotes:
"Nobody can make you feel inferior without your consent."—Eleanor Roosevelt

"Work as though you would live forever, and live as though you would die today."—Og Mandino

My daily affirmation:
This or something better is now manifesting in totally satisfying and harmonious ways for the highest good of all.

## Whose Rooms Are *You* In?

As you build the positive habits of managing your room, it's helpful to reflect on whose rooms you are occupying, where you are in those rooms, and why. Even if they haven't heard of the Who's in Your Room? method, the essential fact of having a relationship with you, of being in your room, means you are in theirs.

There are plenty of times when one value takes precedence over another. For example, even if you believe in being truthful, you can authentically tell some minor falsehoods that make life go smoothly. The great etiquette writer Judith Martin (who wrote as Miss Manners) said, "The problem is with [a] rigid definition of lying." The practical difference between declining an invitation from someone you don't like by saying "I would love to but I can't" (a lie) and telling them "You disgust me" (the truth) is not one of integrity but of intent. Your job in someone else's room is to act with good intent. Real integrity involves weighing the consequences of your actions, acting according to your values, and being accountable for your behavior. In this case, simple kindness is more important than perfect candor.

If you have come willingly into someone's room and over time realize that was a mistake (former partners come to mind), staying in their room in a conducive or positive manner means taking your place and kindly resisting their entreaties for you to come closer. This is tantamount to keeping your own room in order because you are determining how close you need to be. Ultimately, it benefits them too: who needs a person close by who doesn't want to be there?

Let's take that example one step further: a person you dislike persists, trying to draw you closer by inviting you several more times. They don't get the message. Setting limits in this case means stating the message more plainly: "I had fun at that last dinner at your place, but I've decided my room/calendar/ life is just too full now. Thank you for the invitation anyway."

Relationships in life are almost never symmetrical and perfectly balanced. In the give-and-take of relationships, you have to know how much energy someone is demanding of you, whether by attention, loyalty, or some other investment of the breaths you have left.

## Rules of the Room

This book includes a lot of exercises that are presented in a certain order to promote progress as you get your room in order. You don't have to do them all at once, however, and you don't even have to do them in order. Becoming aware of your values, relationships, goals, and inspirations is the work of a lifetime. You might find that your path is cyclical or that you go down unexpected side roads. That's fine because this is *your* room and nobody else's.

## You Can Put Yourself on the Shelf

You have stood on the porch of many, many rooms, asking to be let inside, and you were let into many of those rooms. Since you'll be there forever, you need to ask how you want to inhabit that space. You have gone into many rooms hoping to advance in your career or have a summer romance. You might have entered some of those rooms under false pretenses (you know what they are). In short, you went into some rooms where you didn't belong. What do you do about those?

Put yourself on the shelf.

If you realize that you are exploiting a relationship for what you can get out of it and not putting in anything of value into it, you can back off. Mentally take yourself away from that person and ask how your behavior might change. Perhaps you won't ask for favors quite so much. Perhaps there is still time for you to create a more reciprocal relationship. Maybe they need what you have rather than the other way around.

This is part of living with integrity. When you are in some-one's room purely for your own benefit—something they don't offer freely but you are in effect taking from them by being in their room—step back and reassess if that's how you want to live.

If this is someone with whom you are closely related, a life partner, a business associate, or another close relationship, we offer the principles of your room as a starting point to gain some perspective. It's not our place or our recommendation that you either walk away or beg to be close again. We are suggesting you become clear about that relationship's meaning to you before you force the issue of where you belong in their lives. Perhaps if you are surprised about where you are in their room, you need to consider the reason behind their location in yours.

## Rooms I've Been In: Syd's Story

*Syd Field (1935-2013) was acclaimed as the "guru of all screen-writers" by CNN and "the most sought-after screenwriting teacher in the world" by the* Hollywood Reporter. *His book* Screenplay: The Foundations of Screenwriting *is still consid-ered the bible of the film industry. Syd was inducted into the prestigious Final Draft Hall of Fame in 2006. He shared this story with us a number of years ago.*

Growing up, I and all my friends were more into rebellion than anything else. In high school, we were the guys endlessly in some kind of trouble. But since we were also the star athletes on the track team, we got away with it most of the time. My family still remembers what a concern I became to my mother after my father died when I was twelve. She feared that I wasn't going to make it in life because I was always getting into trouble and I showed no apparent aptitude for anything other than athletics.

By the time we graduated high school, James Dean was a rising star in Hollywood. My friend Frank met Dean by accident, and Jimmy started hanging out with us. My room was our gang. We would stroll down Hollywood Boulevard looking for trouble— and find it we would. We got in a lot of fights and ended up in juvenile hall. We were everything being a rebel was about.

Jimmy Dean somehow found in our room a freedom and another way to look at his life. Instead of living the structured life of an actor, for him, it became the unstructured life of freedom, of which acting was a part. About a year after Jimmy made *Rebel without a Cause*, we realized that our group was the model for the movie's "bad guys," so we started to play that role full on.

And then my mother died—on my birthday. I started to turn my personality around. Out of choice, I didn't continue as the overt, getting-in-trouble, loudmouthed attention-getter. I became the quiet and introverted one. Even though I was a member of the track team at USC the year we became national champions, I decided I would quit athletics.

I went to UC Berkeley and morphed from being a loudmouth attention-getter to a quiet, introverted person who focused on being "good."

At Berkeley, I was drifting, not knowing where I was going and still searching for what I wanted. I started acting and had good success. Then I met my mentor, Jean Renoir, the French film director, screenwriter, actor, producer, and author. He invited me into his room and changed the direction of my life. Renoir said to me, "The future is film—don't waste your time with English literature, don't waste your time trying to be a professional person, the future is film!" He wrote me a letter saying to the UCLA film department, "Let this kid in."

I was at UCLA with Ray Manzarek and Jim Morrison, two guys with a garage band called The Doors. We all made films together and hung out until they went into music and my uncle got me a job as a gofer in the film business. I was still a kid, but I learned I had an unusual gift—I could find stuff. I found the actual Bay of Pigs footage that no one else could locate. I found Grace Kelly's first modeling spread. I found the first film Marilyn Monroe ever made—a Union 76 commercial.

A strange gift, but I had it. I learned that I could find things *if I set my mind to it*. I remember the aha moment when I recognized that I could make the choice to make my room one of success or nonsuccess. That literally changed my life. In that moment, I realized that I could choose the life I wanted.

When I started teaching, I was terrible. I was the worst you can imagine because I had to be the expert, to know more than any of the students and just lecture them. Nobody wanted to be in my room. It got so bad that one day I thought, "Why don't I turn the room upside down?" I opened up the class to answer questions from the students. Out of that experience I realized everyone had the same questions about how to write a screenplay, and that led me to write

*Screenplay*, followed by a lifetime of writing and teaching all over the world.

What's interesting to me is growth. After all these years, I'm still reinventing my role as I am carried along by the current. The self to me is a conscious thing, and any conscious thing lives and grows and changes and adapts to the times. If you don't adapt, it's over. You see that all the time. People who can't adapt get locked in nonsuccess until they perish.

The director Sam Peckinpah invited me into his room and became a wonderful mentor to me. His masterpiece *The Wild Bunch* is about aging western outlaws. All they know how to do is rob banks. But in the story, set in 1913, the world has changed, and they didn't know how to adapt. [Ironically, *The Wild Bunch* changed westerns forever with its revolutionary writing, editing, direction, and graphic violence.] The dilemma of unchanging persons in changing times is really important, and that's exactly what I'm beginning to understand.

I think about this Who's in Your Room? idea in an expanded way by not only having a well-trained doorkeeper and concierge but also by realizing that the rooms I've been in have shaped my life in profound ways. It's not just about who's in my room—it's also about the rooms I enter.

People enter your room, and you enter theirs. Some are mentors and some are antimentors, which we describe in chapter 8. Your world is constantly changing, and you must learn to adapt—to change in the direction of the life you want to live. Syd learned to "turn the room upside down," and his courage to change led to new opportunities and greater success throughout his life.

# 6

# More Tools for Your Room

AT THIS POINT you've assessed who's in your room, identified your values, and read about the lessons some people have learned in their rooms. If you paused to complete the exercises (we hope you have), you have started to master the basic techniques of managing your room. Now it's time to move into some advanced techniques.

## The Lockbox

You're likely to have noticed a fair number of people you would have banned from your room. These are the dealbreakers—the ones you wish hadn't been allowed to enter. You would have no qualms about kicking them to the curb if you could, but you can't because they're already in your room.

Ivan's mother taught him how to deal with such an issue: "Well, we can't quite kick anyone to the curb, but we can box them up and put them on a shelf."

While your doorkeeper becomes more discriminating about the people who want to get into your room, it's time for your concierge to gently escort the worst of the dealbreakers into a special area—the darkest, quietest place in your room. You can envision it as an alcove or nook far off in the back of the room. Or you can think of it as a doorless closet or an old-fashioned steamer trunk. We've found a particularly effective image: the lockbox.

Your concierge can bring any number of people to the lockbox and make sure they go in and don't come out. They don't have a choice because the concierge has the power to sort and move anyone. Once the dealbreaker is inside, the lockbox goes on a shelf. We're talking about a shelf that you need to stand on top of a six-foot ladder to reach. This is not an easy-to-access shelf!

People in there aren't seen or heard, even though they might try to call attention to themselves. Once on that shelf of your metaphorical room, they are unchanged and still never leave the room, but now they and all their baggage are tucked away in a safe place—safe for you.

Mentally relegating these people to the lockbox allows you to regain control over areas of your life that they may have controlled. Put those people and memories in that lockbox, turn the key, and set it on a shelf. Don't let them continue to control your life. Intentionally saying to yourself, "I'm no longer thinking about you," can be wonderfully freeing.

Sorting through the people in your room is an ongoing activity. It helps to use your notebook, but you'll probably know a few people who will go into the lockbox right away. You can even use your list of dealbreakers and sort them into three categories:

- People who absolutely, positively go into the lockbox
- People who go into the lockbox, but you might let them back into the big room later
- People whom you're not quite ready to put there because maybe they can be saved

The word for this sorting is *triage*. Its original meaning is particularly apt for the room. During the Napoleonic Wars, French military surgeons devised a method for separating wounded soldiers into three groups (*triage*) for treatment or evacuation based on the severity of their wounds. Triage gave priority to treating the least endangered soldiers, who were most able to return to their comrades.

Your triage serves the purpose of evacuating the most severely *endangering* people to the lockbox. You don't have to get everyone in there immediately—but take care of the most serious dealbreakers first.

In practice, this means you distance yourself from that person in the best way you can. We'll make suggestions soon about how to do this in the nonmetaphorical world. For now, consider a few tactics to use once you decide someone belongs in that box:

- If someone in your room is obsessively controlling, tell them that you have decided to make your own decisions, full stop. Describe the limits to their control precisely;

for example, "When you tell me that I must spend my money in a certain way, I feel you are appropriating something that is not yours. I will spend my money in the ways I choose."

- If someone is always late and forgetful, describe the behavior and a clear consequence: "I understand that your plans can change, but that does not mean mine have to change with them. The consequence of you never being on time for the carpool is you having to find another way to get to work."

- When someone is addicted to drama and gossip and tries to bring you into it, your concierge can escort them to the lockbox while you make it clear that life is too short to invest your time and life energy into essentially destructive and useless scenes. A warning: You can't participate a little in this and hope they'll understand. Make clear what you think the boundary is between relationship and drama or legitimate information and gossip.

Yes, we're reminding you that you have to live your values moment to moment. Remember, *what consumes your time controls your mind.*

What if someone promises to do better next time? All we can say is *you* get to decide how many "next times" they get before they go into the lockbox. But keep in mind that what you put up with, you end up with.

Here are a few examples of people and the experiences related to them that you can box up—and learn from. You might be writing these kinds of notes to yourself while triaging:

- *A social group*—I thought I'd enjoy joining this book group, but it's not been a valuable experience. Rather than learning from the experience, all I hear is small-town gossip during our meetings. I'll politely quit the group and free up one night a week for someone from whom I can learn.

- *An employee*—I knew when I hired Joe that he would need mentoring, but I'm finding it frustrating to support him when it seems like he doesn't care. He's not getting his job done. More than that, he's late to work consistently—a trait that makes Joe one of my deal-breakers. I'm going to work with HR and give him the opportunity to change. If he can't or won't, I'll move him off my team and make sure his replacement values punctuality and demonstrates ambition.

- *A boss*—I've been putting up with my boss's disorganization and rude remarks for three years, and the situation hasn't improved over time; it's only gotten worse. I'm going to see whether I can switch departments. If that doesn't work, I'll plan my exit strategy from the company by researching my options, networking, and applying to new positions.

- *A grudge*—I resent that my ex has turned my children against me by telling them lies. I am going to move on from that resentment and instead take actions regularly to reconnect with my children to show them I care and love them.

- *Guilt* (this is a big one)—Sometimes I let people in my room out of guilt. Once they are in, I continue to give them attention out of my own guilt. Many times, I tolerate people's behavior out of guilt as well. Guilt does not make for good relationships, and it creates a caustic room. I am not going to feel guilty because of someone else's issues.

- *Family member*—They're family, what can I do? They may be family, and it's true I had no choice about whether they are in my room, but I'm not going to let them run amok in my space any longer.

Is your lockbox beginning to fill up? Don't worry—like your room, it can be any size you like. You don't have to imagine it as a dungeon, either. Maybe it looks more like a cozy hotel room, way up on the shelf, where all those people can live comfortably but can't make you miserable.

---

## Rules of the Room

The lockbox is a tool for managing negative relationships. Remember also to examine all the positive relationships in your room. Let your concierge devote at least as much attention to them as to the toxic people. Soon, those positive people (we call them engines in the next section) will be the majority of people close to you. Isn't that how you want to live?

---

## Recognize Engines and Anchors

Over the years, we've recognized the positive and supportive people whom we want to be around. They focus on solutions in their approach to most problems and are frequently willing to talk through challenges with a positive end in mind. These people are engines. They help us be our best selves, and they motivate us to drive forward in a positive way.

We've also noticed, as we're sure you have, some people complain as though it were an Olympic event. They tend to be negative, argumentative, and obsessed with problems without any realistic help with the solutions. These people are anchors. They hold us back and weigh us down.

The complication with anchors is they typically think of themselves as engines. They are energized by attachment to other people, and yet they stay in one place when you need to move on. They need to be gently escorted to the lockbox.

Engines and anchors are easy to spot by checking how we feel when we're around them (in person, on the phone, through email, or via other means). Does someone make you feel energized, even if you disagree about something? Do you look forward to seeing them and engaging with their particular energy, whether it's sizzling enthusiasm or calm, self-assured competence? They are surely one of your engines. Do you dread a phone call from someone even though they like you? Do you put off answering their emails? That's a pretty good clue they're an anchor.

Tap into your reactions. If you become aware of resenting their presence, they are probably an anchor, and you can practice letting go with rituals such as the lockbox exercise above. Or you might admit that your resentment is not about them, but about your own behavior.

Resentment is a strong tip-off that an anchor is tying you down. As the saying goes, resentment is the poison you take hoping to kill the other person. It's a strong and toxic emotion attached to unresolved relationships or events. This happens a lot with family members, for example, when you find yourself exaggerating the injury someone caused you. In that case, the exercise might make you aware that you are holding on to that self-justifying resentment. If you find yourself playing the victim, you might want to create a similar ritual: put that part of you in the lockbox. (This in no way minimizes real injuries that people have caused you. Who owes whom an apology is entirely your decision. The point is to let resentment prompt an awareness of what's going on in that room between your ears.)

Through rituals like this, you make your room more spacious and freer for the people, things, and activities that are good for you. In time, you make room in your mind and heart to see those people more fully.

Look at your list of who's in your room again. Who jumps out as an engine? Who is an anchor? Are they in their right places? Your engines should be close, your anchors, not so much.

## Mastering the Art of Benign Neglect

You get more of what you want by becoming aware of what you're focusing on. A good friend of ours, Mark McKergow, said, "If all you focus on is the problem, you become an expert on the problem. But, if you focus on the solution, you become an expert on the solution."

By working with your doorkeeper and concierge, clearly focusing on what you do want rather than what you don't, you will create your own luck and opportunities. To the extent that you're clear about what you want, it will show up in your life. As it does and you welcome it into your room, the elements of your existence that you'd rather be without will fade into the distant background as a result of your not paying them attention. We call this the *benign neglect* approach to room management.

This new context for your life allows you to mentally and emotionally move elements from the foreground to the background. Those troublesome people and events that have had starring roles in the story of your life become mere dots in the distance. For the truly troublesome people, they go in the lockbox and on the shelf so you rarely think of them. In this way, you create space for what you actually want featured in the foreground of your life.

Benign neglect takes many forms. It's any decision you make that allows a person in your room (or an activity associated with that person) to move toward the back or be gently put in the lockbox without harming them. That in turn allows someone else to step a little bit closer to you. In other words, you're making room for people and experiences that add value and joy to your life. Often benign neglect is unintentional— perhaps a byproduct of not managing your room well and with purpose. Maybe you've accidentally let a friendship wane by not devoting any time to it. But other times, benign neglect can be intentional and progressive—a direct result of managing your room purposefully. It can be a deliberate strategy. Here are some examples of how to use benign neglect:

- Tell someone no. (See chapter 7 for ways to say no without sounding like a jerk.)

- Don't engage someone who is looking for a fight.
- Suggest that instead of holding weekly in-person meetings with a colleague, you have virtual meetings every other week.
- Maintain membership in an organization but no longer hold a leadership role.
- Speak with a friend when she calls but initiate a call to her only once a month.
- Opt out of pub night or wine night in favor of staying in with your spouse or partner.
- Don't respond to phone calls or emails quite so quickly.

We've seen that benign neglect can be helpful to the person on whom it's focused. If an anchor person is using you as an excuse to complain about a problem without changing it, you're taking that excuse away. You are inviting them to become more independent or accountable for their situation. In some cases, benign neglect is the best thing you can do for someone else, such as when you stop enabling a person with an addiction problem or indulging an adult child who wants you to take their side in a disagreement with a sibling.

The bottom line here is that benign neglect works, even if you do it by accident. We're suggesting that, when appropriate, you do it by design. It can be done progressively, meaning that you gradually move into benign neglect over time. It doesn't have to happen overnight.

# Ignore the Grenade

*A friend shares this story of benign neglect in their family.*

A relative would come to big family events, and every time, she'd toss a verbal grenade into the crowd. She would say something so outrageous that it would blow up the event. Everyone would react with anger and escalate. She ruined one family event after another.

The rest of the family was on the verge of saying, "You're not welcome anymore," but they didn't want to do that because, after all, she was *family*. Finally, someone suggested, "We need to tell her this is no longer okay. Even if it doesn't make a difference, we have to draw a line in the sand. More than that, we have to change our reaction." They all agreed that they wouldn't engage with the grenade thrower.

The next time this woman came to an event and threw her verbal hand grenade, everyone turned to her and said, "Oh, hmmm, okay." And then turned back to their own conversation. At the next event, same thing: the verbal hand grenade was followed by a bored, "Oh, hmmm, okay." This happened a few times until she stopped coming to the dinners and events. When she returned later, she behaved herself.

Just ignoring the bad behavior and not engaging with her made all the difference. It took all the energy out of her assaults. This version of benign neglect defused every grenade.

# The Lockbox Ritual

We invite you to create a ritual to signify putting someone in the lockbox. When you decide someone belongs there, find their names in your notebook or on your dealbreakers list, and reflect on the reasons you need to put them away by completing these sentences as if you were talking directly to them:

- You are going into the lockbox (or corner or alcove) because _____.
- In the past, when you did _____, I felt _____.
- I let you into my room because _____ _____.
- The good consequences of letting you in were _____ _____.
- The harmful consequences of letting you in were _____ _____.
- By putting you there, I promise myself to _____ _____.
- In the future, I will remember what you have taught me about letting similar people into my room. That might happen when _____.
- My wish for you is _____ _____.

Complete each sentence thoughtfully. Don't excuse your behavior or gloss over theirs. Thank them for any contributions they might have made to your life, even if they only taught you not to let people like them in.

This thought process will allow you to then circle back to your doorkeeper to make sure no other similar people or experiences enter your room. Your lockbox, benign neglect, rituals, and strategies to distinguish engines from anchors all have something in common: saying no to someone or something so you have more room to say yes to people who matter. That's what the next chapter is about. But first, a friend shares why it's so hard to say no at all.

## Why We Have Trouble Saying No: Lynne's Story

*Lynne Twist is the author of the bestselling, award-winning book* The Soul of Money: Transforming Your Relationship with Money and Life.

There's a reason people have trouble saying no. When I feel I might be trying to spread myself too thin and do too much, I have to examine carefully what pulls me toward a project and sift through the lies and myths that surround it. It's easy to keep saying yes to every call to help and thinking it takes more work to say no, but staying seated in reality is what keeps the number of projects in my room manageable.

What I have come to see is that we live in what I call a *lie of scarcity*—a condition of scarcity rooted in a whole network of lies. Of course, a network of lies is a strong term, but I actually mean it. Nineteenth-century humorist Josh Billings reportedly said, "It ain't what a man don't know that makes him a fool, but what he does know that ain't so." This is the nature of the network of lies.

There rampantly exists an unconscious, unexamined mindset that generates behaviors inconsistent with our humanity. This is not about *what* you think but *where* you are thinking from. It's almost like viewing the world through a lens or filter so that everything you see is altered by the unconscious, unexamined mindset from which you are thinking. Consequently, even before thinking, deliberating, or making a decision, there is this filter of perception that everything is scarce and you must have more.

This mindset of scarcity is a total trap. This is distinct from the reality that there are people who don't have enough to eat, who don't have access to clean water, who don't have adequate housing, and who in this sense really don't have enough. I've spent a good portion of my life working with people like this. I'm not talking about them. I'm talking about people primarily in affluent countries where there is this unconscious, unexamined mindset that drives aberrant behavior and the unconscious, unexamined belief in scarcity, which contains three toxic myths.

The first toxic myth is made of two parts. The first is that there is not enough—not enough time, money, energy, sex, sleep, weekends, Tuesdays, Wednesdays. There are not enough hours in the day and not enough hours in the night. There is just this relentless consideration that there's not enough of anything. It's become the tyranny we live in.

The second part of toxic myth number one is that there is not enough to go around and someone, somewhere, will always be left out. This is devastating and ultimately fatal.

It creates an *us* and a *them*, and it legitimizes accumulating way more than you need to ensure that you and yours are never among those who are left out.

This mythology is unwittingly taught to us very early when we go to our first birthday party and start playing musical chairs. In the beginning it seems like such a harmless game—happy little kids and loving parents—and when in the first round or two, as a chair is withdrawn, you don't really notice that someone gets left out because you're focused on how you got a chair. But as they take a chair away and then there's another round and then they take a chair away and then there's another round, suddenly there are more kids without chairs than kids with chairs. And of course, the kid who wins the game is always the most aggressive one who will push anyone out of the way to get their chair.

While this sounds like an innocently simple game, it is almost a training program for the world in which we live, where you can do almost anything to anyone to make sure that you don't get left out. It is now amplified to gargantuan proportions in some of these reality TV shows, which are based on the same model—the winner-take-all model—every episode a metaphorical chair gets kicked out and somebody gets left out and leaves the show.

The second toxic myth, flowing directly from the first, is that more of anything and everything is better—more square feet in your house is better, more boats, more planes, more this, more that. It's not that more isn't sometimes useful and important. This insatiable, constant obsession with getting more makes no sense. And it's toxic because the drive is totally unconscious. This more-is-always-better mentality is driven and reinforced by constant messages. Analysts tell us we see a minimum of around three thousand advertisements a day (more if you spend a lot of time on social media), telling us we need more of something we have or we have to get something we don't have in order to be okay. If we live in an urban area, it can be up to tens of thousands of messages a day, which is overwhelming.

The third toxic myth is that it's just the way it is. This is really the worst one because it's a source of resignation, of giving up, or of feeling like there is nothing you can do to make a difference. It's a source of depression, disappointment, and discouragement. Here we are, living in the richest country on earth, and we have also accumulated the greatest amount of debt in the history of the world. This is what happens when you place a greater value on outer riches than inner riches.

Lynne's statement reminds us that acquiring people in your room, like acquiring wealth or fame, can be driven by an unconscious but dangerous mindset—the lie of scarcity.

The lie of scarcity can keep you trapped for life in a never-ending quest to satisfy the next wish, the next need, the next responsibility. You can step away from this in your room and every corner of your life; the choice is yours.

# 7

# The Liberating Power
# of Saying No

A SMART management consultant told us years ago, "Trying to manage the amount of work you have to do is useless. There will always be too much. Instead, focus on managing your *capacity*. If you are clear about your limits, you won't typically have too much to do."

Albert Einstein had a related belief. On a visit to Boston in 1921, the great physicist was asked, "What is the speed of sound?" He answered that he did not carry such information in his mind because it was readily available in books. For all his brilliance, he didn't clutter up his mind with unnecessary information. In fact, keeping his mind uncluttered *contributed* to his brilliance.

Your room is like that. Even though it contains everyone you've let in, making it almost infinitely large, only so many people can come near enough to interact with you. Your capacity for meaningful relationships is limited because you're human.

Given that fact, you need to consider what you'll do with your limited capacity.

The Oxford psychology professor Robin Dunbar calculated that human beings can maintain about 150 relationships at a time. His work has stood up to thirty years of scrutiny, much of it by people who say, "Wait a minute, I know a lot more people than that!" There are a lot more people than that in your room, right? But Dunbar's number is about *meaningful relationships*—about 150 meaningful relationships at any one time. Many people in your room were good friends long ago but you haven't been in touch with them for years. (There they are, way at the back of the room. Reading these words, you're probably remembering a few.) You also might have made a close friend recently, and they are nearby, definitely in the ranks of your 150 current friends. Our point is that your capacity for the number of *real* relationships that you have is limited. After people get over their shock, they see that this makes sense from a purely quantitative point of view. Meaningful relationships take time and attention. Being human, you have limited time and attention to give. Even if you know a thousand people, remember Dunbar's number.

Before you say yes to people, activities, and responsibilities, gauge your capacity in terms of time you can devote to someone. If you say yes to everyone who asks, "Got a minute?" you will run out of minutes. Instead, learn the power of addition by subtraction: by saying no to certain things, you create more room for the things to which your heart and soul truly want to say yes.

When you learn to say no to some people as well as to your self-appointed expectations, you will still be busy, but your life will be full of the things that fill your cup instead of the things that drain it dry.

You will also learn to judge your metaphorical capacity to carry what people want to give you. The real tragedy isn't having too much to do; the real tragedy is choosing to do things without a wholehearted devotion and conscious alignment with your own purpose. This is not a scarcity mindset; it's accepting the fact that your time and attention are finite and then acting on that fact.

## Rules of the Room

Some people just won't take no for an answer. Before you give up and let them get their hooks in, we suggest that maybe they need a longer answer.

You can say, "Before we go into this again, there's something you need to know. I imagine my life as a big room, and in that room is everyone who is meaningful to me. I know that I can have a real relationship with only about 150 of them at a time—that's just a fact of life. You are in my room, and you will always be there. But I have to make choices about who is close to me in that room and who is farther away. You should know that you are farther away than others."

If they persist, you can even tell them about the doorkeeper that let them in and explain that the concierge is inviting them to step a little farther away. And if they still persist—some people are just stubborn that way—you can use one of the suggested ways of saying no below.

In some of the stories in this book, people tell how they explained their room. You might want to highlight those answers and use them yourself.

## Setting Boundaries

In chapter 4, you listed some of the behaviors that are unacceptable to you—the signals that someone is a dealbreaker. How you act once you've determined someone is a dealbreaker can make the difference between success and failure in managing your life in the room. The term for this is *setting boundaries*. If you do not do this, it will be easy for you to be so crowded by dealbreaker behavior that you become lost, even though it's your room. Many people are unaware of other people's limits and will force their behaviors on you if you do not stand your ground.

How do you set boundaries? The simple answer is saying no.

In a life that offers a thousand choices a day (we mean that literally), saying no is the only way to navigate all the temptations and traps that demand our attention. *No* gets a bad rap from people who believe it's possible to have it all. If you want to have it all, we suggest you aren't choosing wisely between what truly feeds your life and what wants to drain the life out of you. Face it, saying no leaves you more room in your life for the right yes.

When you set boundaries by saying no, you set in motion a strategy called *behavioral disruption*. Behavioral disruption starts with communication, not confrontation. Clear, open, honest, and direct communication is almost always the best way to address issues. To do this, speak with the person about the issue and share what your response will be the next time one of your dealbreakers is broken. This signals you will disrupt the unacceptable behavior. If the person then crosses the boundary you have set, remove yourself.

Our friend Rick Sapio used to have mixed feelings every time he picked up the phone for his regularly scheduled calls with his mother because she would *always* start complaining so harshly that some people would consider it verbal assault. Finally, he decided he would tell his mother that he loved his regular calls with her but was uncomfortable when she focused so much on this negativity. He said that, from then on, when she launched into one of these controversies, he was going to politely let her know that he needed to go. He'd calmly say goodbye, and he would hang up. After doing just that two or three times in a row, it almost never happened again. Rick set boundaries and then adhered to them.

Setting boundaries means saying no to a specific behavior. You're not putting people in the lockbox (yet). You are pointing out behaviors that harm your relationship. If you want to include your room metaphor, you can say, "When you complain on our calls, I need to move you farther back in the room of my life because it's crowding out the love I feel for you."

Don't expect people to instantly thank you for setting boundaries. If you stick to them, however, something magical can happen. All that time they spent doing things that are unacceptable to you can now get filled with more meaningful behaviors and conversations. When you say no, you give people the opportunity to see what their behavior costs them. That person who habitually complains might decide to talk about what they're happy about, maybe something as simple as a concert they saw on television recently or what they are planning for their garden next year. You can help this process by prompting them with questions once your boundaries are clear.

Managing the people who are already in your room can be less stressful than you may think. If you put a little thought into how you want to handle different types of situations, you'll be less likely to be caught off guard and inadvertently let someone else take control of your room. When you're able to handle the people in your room in a way that adds value to your life rather than creates obstacles or stress, you'll find you're on your path to a more fulfilling life.

Thinking through these kinds of situations in advance will truly help you. Often, when people are dealing with stressful interpersonal relationships and they haven't really thought through their responses, they come across as sarcastic, angry, or unfeeling. Sometimes they panic and tell the concierge to throw that annoying person in the lockbox, put them on the shelf, and forget about them. It's natural to give these impressions when you react to situations you haven't thought through.

You don't have to subject yourself to drama anymore. This can be a life-changing experience. If you do the work and trust the process, you'll be glad you did. We're guessing you'll come back to this chapter from time to time for a reminder of the power of saying no.

## A Therapist's Advice

We don't recommend having an angry confrontation with someone who violates your boundaries. Therapists and professional negotiators suggest a tool that shifts the focus from what they want to what you need. You do this with a simple formula: "When you do *this*, I feel *that*."

In our example of Rick and his mother, that simple formula would be "When you spend the phone call complaining, I feel you are treating me like a therapist, paid to listen to your troubles" or "Mom, when you complain about your life, I feel frustrated that all the efforts of me and my siblings to help you are never enough to make you feel satisfied."

To a boss or business partner who sends emails at ten o'clock at night and expects an immediate answer, you can say, "When you expect me to answer nonemergency questions at night, I feel torn between being there for my family and doing my job. That is frustrating, and I end up resenting both. I will answer your emails in the morning."

## The Door Is Your Front Line for Saying No

Your doorkeeper can help at this front line of your life. Go back to your list of values, both the values you live now and your aspirational ones. Knowing what you know now, ask yourself some probing questions. Would you choose to do business with that associate? Would you try to be a closer connection to that friend? Would you even let that neighbor in the door? With a bit of introspection, you can learn to make different choices in the future. This reflection is part of training your doorkeeper to guard the door based on your values.

What about the people you might want to let in later? They could be an acquaintance at work or a person you had one good conversation with at a party and who is asking for your phone number. It could be someone who is associated with your business, so you have a bit in common but you don't know yet whether they're a dealmaker, a dealbreaker, or someone in between.

Ivan gets a lot of invitations from these folks because he founded BNI. Even though he's no longer responsible for day-to-day operations, he regularly gets invitations from members to connect. They might not think much about it, but they just want to be connected to the founder. Ivan also has many people he has to deal with to get something done, but he doesn't want anything more than a transactional relationship with them. You have people like this in your life—people you see regularly on your commute or on a volunteer committee. They might be fine people, but they don't belong in your room.

When this happens, Ivan decides that the person remains outside for the time being but is not exactly turned away. They are outside the door but on the porch. His attitude is "I don't want to let you into my room because I don't know enough about you. I don't want to let you in only to make the concierge put you on the shelf. Right now, you belong on the porch."

There are some simple ways to redirect people. If they are asking for a favor, refer them to someone more qualified or more able to help.

## Saying the Right Yes: Stephen's Story

*Stephen Josephs is an executive coach, author, and consultant particularly interested in the intersection between business performance, psychology, and mind-body disciplines. He has embraced a daily practice of mind-body disciplines for more than four decades (e.g., tai chi, qigong, aikido, meditation). He is a wonderful humorist, excellent classical guitarist, and celebrant of the human spirit.*

My doorkeeper is a talent scout. He looks for individuals who want to come at challenges and opportunities in ways they haven't considered before. They need to be open to experiment with new ways of thinking and, perhaps more importantly, refine their capacity to pay attention. They're the ones I want to fill my room. When I coach these kinds of leaders, they get the most from what I uniquely offer, and it brings out the best in both of us.

Not selecting everyone who comes along is not so much about saying no to some people but saying yes to the right people.

That's why I invest a great deal of time qualifying potential coaching clients. I offer risk-free sessions so I can deeply understand them. Anyone who visits my website can fill out a form requesting one of these sessions, but I don't automatically accept everyone. This care and attention has been the secret of my success and happiness in my work. When I look at my calendar and see the names of clients I will talk to, I look forward to every one of those conversations. To me that's heaven. These are the people I have said yes to.

I don't worry about refusing people. It can be just the right thing. It certainly was for me when I ran into a friend's fierce and implacable doorkeeper.

In the early '80s my wife and I had been living in an ashram where we practiced hours of yoga and meditation on a daily basis. I was also a seminar leader, and I had a friend in that business, David Gordon, whom I loved dearly. David was a wonderful neuroloinguistic-programming trainer, but even more important for me, he enjoyed the inherent hilarity of life. We spent hours together laughing ourselves silly.

One day I phoned him because I had a perfect idea for a workshop we could do together. I asked whether he was interested in what I'd cooked up. David said, "I heard a story, and I need to ask you about it first." He proceeded to tell me about an incident involving my yoga teacher, who used to run training camps for women in the summer in Española, New Mexico.

One of my close friends attended that camp when she was in the first trimester of her pregnancy. Because of doing strenuous yoga at that altitude, she miscarried. My friend wanted other women to benefit from what she had learned the hard way: there is substantial risk in doing kundalini yoga at that altitude early on in their pregnancy. She told a member of the yogi's staff what had happened. Rather than dealing with her compassionately, the yogi publicly excoriated her. In front of a large gathering of women, he told her she lost her baby because of her own selfishness and ego, and it had nothing to do with his yoga.

David asked me whether the story was true. I said yes. Then he asked whether I had stood up for my friend in any way. I weaseled around a bit. "I wasn't there at the time," I said, "and I tried to work with her later." "But did you," he asked, "stand up for her?" I said, "No." David said, "Then I won't appear on any public stage with you."

David's pronouncement felt like an arrow through my heart. At the same time, it felt right, and I told him so. After

I hung up, I turned to my wife, Alice, and said, "Give me one good reason why we're still here." Two weeks later we departed the cult we had lived in for twelve years.

Think of it this way. Saying no to some people leaves you space in your room to open the door to say yes to other people, the right yes.

Whether they're scouting talent or choosing who gets in your room, a good doorkeeper benefits everyone. When we let them do their job, we end up living in a place that is truly our home.

## How to Say No without Sounding Like a Jerk (or Worse)

Someone wants to come into your room. Or someone's already there and wants to come up close to you. And you're thinking, "Oh no you don't!" You might want to say it aloud, but the trouble with that is, they then think you're a jerk (or worse). Now you are opponents, trapped in the room. Maybe they'll go away, or maybe they'll pressure you to relent.

There's another way to handle this than the direct "No you don't" answer. Develop a set of responses like the ones in the following list. Ivan likes to say, "Diplomacy is the art of letting someone else have your way." You can say no without burning bridges. Creating enemies by saying "Hell no!" is not the way to manage your room.

Here's a baker's dozen of ways to say no without sounding like a jerk:

- Say, "No, thank you."
- Tell them, "If I said yes, I'm afraid I'd let you down. I want you to succeed, and I can't do this for you as well as someone else."
- If you want someone in your room, but they want to bring in a lot of baggage, you can tell them to leave their baggage outside (one version of setting boundaries).
- If they are already in your room (a family member, for example), you can name their baggage and have the concierge take it outside. Your brother-in-law might be in your room, but his credit card debt belongs on the porch. (We'll say more about managing family members in chapter 9.)
- If everyone has access to your time, it gets used up, and there's nothing left, not just for you but also for the people in your room whom you love and who deserve your time. That's another capacity problem, so say, "My capacity to help/listen/wait is completely used up, and you must find someone with time."
- Learn to explain your doorkeeper to others: for example, you can say, "I would never hang up on you! My doorkeeper did!" And then—because you respect them or just because you're a good person—explain the room to them.
- Say, "I'll listen to what you have to say. But when the discussion is over, the answer will probably be no." (We use this when a relative or friend asks for money.)
- Say, "If I allow you into my room, I will immediately regret the amount of time and energy I will have to spend getting my concierge to move you away. It's best if we don't start."

- Say, "If I allow you into my room and close to me, I'll have to push someone else back. I am careful to have people close who can make a mutually beneficial, warm, and equal relationship. Right now, those seats are all taken."
- Say, "I understand that what you offer (or sell) has value to you, but it doesn't have enough value for me. You have misjudged my values and/or needs, and you must find someone else who shares them with you."
- Say, "Poor planning on your part does not create an emergency for me. You cannot come into my room, but you can take away that observation."
- Say, "In my room, people are so close that they can catch each other's contagious parts. I'm afraid your anger/worry/habits are contagious, and I don't want anybody, least of all me, to catch them."
- And finally—don't Seinfeld it. In the *Seinfeld* television series, characters would go off on some crazy, complicated subterfuge or ruse and end up getting into more trouble than if they'd been candid to begin with. You can be polite and still be direct.

Reread each of these slowly. Many of them will remind you of the situations and people who work their way into your room because you said yes. You said yes even when you had that nagging little voice at the back of your mind saying, "This is not a good idea. Remember what happened last time. Please find a way to say no!"

That voice? That's the experienced voice of your concierge telling you (and your doorkeeper) that, in the end, it's really better for everyone if you find a way to say no. Otherwise, sooner or later you'll be telling your concierge they were right, and somebody needs to go into the lockbox.

When you say no, hold your ground. Don't escalate. Instead, simply rephrase your answer slightly. This works well over email. For example, you could respond with "Thanks, but I'm not taking on any new clients for my tax business at this time." And if they repeat their request, reply with "I had to stop accepting new clients two years ago. Thanks again for asking. You might look at this directory of local tax preparers" and include a link to that resource.

We have one last crucial suggestion: try not to feel guilty for saying no. Although we love to say yes as often as possible, sometimes the cost of saying yes is too great. In these cases, try to be at peace with your decision to say no and realize you are protecting entry into your room. Say no and then move on knowing that you made the right decision for you.

## Giving Away Your Power

➡️ This exercise can be done many times, and we suggest you return to it periodically because it keeps producing new insights. That way your room will stay fresh and dynamic as you learn to say no to the person who keeps letting the wrong people in—yourself.

There are a thousand reasons for letting the wrong people in when you know better. Maybe you were trying to get something from them. Maybe you're related, and you think you have no choice. Maybe somebody in your room invited them without asking you (don't let that person get past your doorkeeper).

At the top of a page in your notebook, write "Why I let [NAME] in when I knew better."

Then, before you list all their terrible behaviors and toxic effects on you and your room, pause and listen to that quiet voice of your concierge telling you this isn't the first time this has happened. What did you think you would get from letting them in? Approval? A feeling that you're a good person? A possible business deal? A favor to a friend? Keep writing. If you like, you can separate your reasons into "things I got that I wanted" (approval) and "things I avoided that I didn't want" (guilt).

If you can think of a time this happened before—which is what your concierge is telling you—what was the outcome? Did things work out great, or did your concierge end up marching that person and their baggage all the way to the back of the room?

The takeaway from this exercise is simple: how much power are you giving others to determine your happiness? If you are doing this, why? We tend to give power away in small doses through attachment, obligations, promises, and assumed responsibilities. We need to identify those relationships and moments in order to take power back by saying no.

## Learning to Say No: Libby's Story

*Elizabeth "Libby" Scheele is a Minnesotan artist who found her creative wings had been clipped by her taking on too much. What is worse, she realized she was the one to blame. She could not say no to others. She needed to do something about it.*

Before I had a doorkeeper, my room was like the waiting room in an emergency room. I always seemed to be admitting one too many emergencies after another. The problem was I had been addicted to yes, and learning to say no is not so easy. Now I'm constantly performing triage in an attempt to restore order to it all.

I am a wonderful nurturer. Too good. That was the problem. I was taking on too many people and projects, and my own work suffered. I'd get a burst of creative energy, and I would be so busy that I couldn't listen to it, and I couldn't be present for it, so what could come of it never happened.

Since being introduced to the doorkeeper and the idea of a room that is held sacred, I finally feel that my life has taken the direction I always wanted it to take. I have started to say, "No thank you," to many more projects than ever before. This has freed me to focus on the people and projects that I am most passionate about. My creativity flows, and everybody wins.

People are comfortable asking me for help, especially my husband, and I love being available for him. I also love being available for my family and my community. At the same time, I feel there are things that are supposed to come through me and into this world, and I have to do them. I absolutely have to do them.

So I have to practice making the distinction between opportunities and distractions. What I have taught myself is to take one event at a time with the understanding that just because I am related to a person, and just because I have spent a huge amount of time with them over the years, it doesn't mean that person or their project can demand my attention.

I listen to people carefully now as they give me an invitation or offer me what they believe is an opportunity. Then I tell them how much I appreciate their thoughtfulness—I always make sure they know I am grateful. I let some of these people know that they can be in my room but they cannot bring a project with them, and they have to be very quiet if they are going to be in the room. I am simply establishing boundaries so I have time that is mine to express my passion through projects that profoundly matter to me. I am always very mindful of being kind when I decline a project, meeting, or social event.

Initially, my fear was that once my doorkeeper, concierge, and I got busy, I would start to feel less connected. I thought that if I said no to people, I would be sitting in my room all by myself in dead silence. But what I understand now is that I am doing what I am supposed to be doing, and by graciously putting my doorkeeper in place, people can see this and feel connected to me in some way. They are not fretting over what I am not doing with them.

I just spent a couple of hours with my eighty-seven-year-old neighbor. I play cribbage with him every week. Today he wanted to play one more game, and I said to him, "Leonard, I really have to go home right now. The light is perfect, and I need to finish the painting I am working on, but I will see you on Sunday." And he was fine with this. Before I would've said, "Well, okay, one more game." Before, on some level I believed I was keeping him alive. Now I realize that he may be just fine on his own.

Learning to say no to the distractions means you can make room to say yes to the most important opportunities. Setting simple limits, even on healthy activities like visiting a neighbor, is a discipline you can practice any moment of the day.

# 8

# Joys and Pitfalls of Your Room

OVER YEARS, we've observed common experiences among the people who have applied the Who's in Your Room? question to their lives. Like any skill, it takes practice and repetition for you to develop this strategy into a healthy habit. That takes time. It will take less time, however, if you think deeply about the joys and pitfalls that come with managing your room. This chapter is a guide to moments or themes in your life when asking the question becomes a life-changing experience.

You will develop the habit of noticing when you want to let someone in and where that urge comes from. You will automatically think of making healthy choices. When someone wants to come into your life (and thus into your room), you will pause from saying yes or no immediately and consider what it would mean to have them in there. Your doorkeeper will become more alert and discriminating about who has a claim on your time, life, and attention. Your concierge will become more alert to the times someone in your room needs to be gently but firmly escorted farther away or even put up on the shelf.

We think of habits like those in this wonderful quotation from Og Mandino: "I have surrendered my free will to the years of accumulated habits, and the past deeds of my life have already marked out a path which threatens to imprison my future. . . . Therefore, if I must be a slave to habit let me be a slave to good habits. My bad habits must be destroyed, and new furrows prepared for good seed."

In chapter 4, we noted that dealbreakers can be especially memorable, and so we started with them and later described dealmakers. When it comes to describing the joys and pitfalls of your room, we will begin with the positive observations first.

## Joys

You can find joy just by bringing more positive people into your room. They are loving, inspiring, talented, accomplished, or in other ways role models. That includes people who have done the work of mastery—whether in playing a musical instrument, preparing a meal, writing a poem, or offering a well-reasoned point of view—as well as members and sponsors.

### Masters

Mastery is a subject so compelling and complex that you can fill a library of books describing it. We are interested, but not convinced, in simple formulas like "practice something for ten thousand hours and you'll get great at it." (If that were universally true, Doug would be a scratch golfer. He is not.) Mastery arises from the interplay of aptitude, intent, physical and mental capability, dedication, hard work, and the ineffable quality of grace.

The psychologist Mihaly Csikszentmihalyi, in his masterful book *Flow: The Psychology of Optimal Experience,* described a state of unselfconscious concentration on an activity. You see that state in a child at play, champion athlete, or chess grandmaster. People who cultivate that state are working on mastery, even if they might not describe it that way. Who is more masterful at play than a child?

Mastery leads to both achievement and fulfillment. The relationship one makes with an activity over the long time it takes to achieve mastery creates a desire to keep improving that can never be exhausted. This state has many different expressions among the most accomplished; one of our favorites is the quotation "I am still learning," often attributed to Michelangelo but uttered by other greats, such as Muhammad Ali.

Thomas Keller, the founder of The French Laundry (which serious critics believe is one of America's top five restaurants), knows how good a chef he is, but told Stewart, "If you are a good cook, and you have access to better ingredients than I do, you'll be a better chef than me on that day." His frank observation shifted our perspective on his particular mastery. Keller is a master who understands that the experience he creates is the sum of many parts, a humbling observation that drives him to seek perfection in every detail of his work.

Are there masters in your room? When you appreciate their gifts and diligence, do you automatically switch to comparison mode, saying things such as, "I could never speak in public so effectively," "I'll never play jazz guitar like that," or "There's no way I can develop her financial genius." If that's what you do, you are wasting the precious resource of their example. Instead of comparison, become a student of their gifts and especially their attitude toward the work they love.

We cannot tell you what activities to love or even if you should try to master something that's hard. Instead, we urge you to consider people you know who are incredibly good at something and consider how you can apply what they believe and what they do to the things you love to do. Be alert to the temptations to compare yourself to or imitate them. Your mastery is almost certainly different from theirs.

To understand your relationship to mastery, take out your notebook and interview each of the people you would call a master. Yes, we're asking you to talk to them about it.

- What are they masterful at?
- What does being a master—or continuing to grow as a master—mean to them?
- What are their habits of mastery (e.g., practicing every day, studying)?
- What is their attitude toward mastery—humble, proud, challenged, energized?
- Whom are the masters they admire?

## Mentors and Sponsors

Mentors are among the most significant people in anyone's room. They might be teachers you knew long ago, parents, coaches, managers, or friends who helped you move forward in your life. You typically hear about mentors in the course of business, such as the senior partner in a law firm who selects a few promising (or struggling) young associates and continues their education informally, teaching them skills and savvy that the mentor has acquired through long experience.

A retired college president we know describes a special kind of mentor in business or education that she calls *a sponsor*. A sponsor is not just a source of advice and support, such as a mentor, but also actively creates opportunities for you. In business, they would suggest you work on projects that would stretch you beyond your current responsibilities or even expertise, saying, "You can do this, even if it's a steep learning curve. Now go be bad at something for a while, and you'll get better at it quickly." In your room, sponsors will bring themselves close to you on their own. They are energized by giving away their own expertise or influence to others. The role of sponsor is great for elders who have succeeded in any walk of life and want to pay that back, making a tangible difference in the lives of others. You'll definitely want to let them into your room.

Keep in touch with your teachers and advisors! They can be lifelong mentors. We know a distinguished economist who spent months trying to solve a complex set of partial differential equations for a paper he was writing. He happened to mention his struggles with this problem in an email to his old math advisor. The advisor promptly wrote back, "Well, if you've tried a power series expansion and that didn't work, I don't know what to suggest." Of course, the power series approach was the key to the solution, and the economist went on to publish the paper to great success.

We've also found that many people have virtual mentors whom they might not have met face-to-face but who have had a profound impact on them. They might be philosophers, artists, musicians, or historical figures such as Saint Augustine, Shakespeare, or the Stoics. They might be business influencers like Peter Drucker or social or political leaders like Reverend Martin Luther King Jr. or Ronald Reagan. Virtual mentors highlight the fact that much of our experience is subjective; even without real contact, you might form an emotional relationship with them through their influence on you and your beliefs.

How can Saint Augustine or the Stoics, who lived centuries ago, be your virtual mentors? If you apply their ideas enthusiastically to your life, then yes, your doorkeeper has brought them into your room. If mentors like them are in your mind—especially if they are doing you good—they are in your room. There are millions who would say that one or more of the great saints, teachers, sages, and philosophers is a powerful force in their rooms.

Alice Waters is a master not only of cooking but of rethinking Americans' whole relationship to food and the food system. One day she mentioned her virtual mentor, saying, "He's a man who's passed now and whom I never met, but he wrote a book on an approach to food and cooking. His essential ideas have stayed with me throughout my culinary career." Waters in turn has been a real-life mentor to many of our finest, most innovative chefs—and no doubt a virtual mentor to generations of cooks.

One small caution when considering mentors: you might be overinvested in people you revere and admire. You can create an idealized vision of them and your relationship. They too are human beings with faults and shortcomings, and if you don't see them as they are in relation to you, you can develop a distorted view of them, bringing them closer than they should be.

Do you have mentors, or have you had them in the past? Make a list of their names and answer these questions:

- Who are your mentors?
- Why did you choose to allow each other into your rooms?
- What do you receive from them, and what do you give them?
- Have you thanked them or told them what their mentoring did for you?
- Are they in the right place in your room today, or does that need to change?
- Who are your virtual mentors?

Are you a mentor to someone? They're in your room too, so they go on your list of mentoring relationships.

## Rules of the Room

There are mentors, and there are *antimentors*—people who teach us what *not* to do by their example. When Doug does workshops on management, he holds a competition for people to tell their *worst* boss story. At the end of the stories, the room gets to vote on who had the worst boss. Hands shoot up, and people talk about bosses who belittled them, made terrible decisions, or hired their own relatives. Bosses who ran once-great businesses into the ground. Bosses who sucked all the life out of the culture and awarded themselves big bonuses. We bet you can write a great bad-boss story in your notebook right now (go ahead).

Writer and technologist Kevin Kelly put it well on his blog, *The Technium*: "Don't ever work for someone you don't want to become."

Antimentors have a way of teaching us our values by contrast (more about that in the next chapter). They're in your room, but they definitely belong in the lockbox on the shelf.

A friend suggests that while you're listing your antimentors, you might also label some of them *tormentors*—the worst of the worst.

---

## *Busyness*

Busyness exists on the borderline between a joy and a pitfall. Are you always busy, always expanding your to-do list of obligations to people? When Ivan speaks to BNI gatherings, that's the number one reason people say their lives are chaotic. He suggests that they shift their mindset to help unclutter their mental rooms.

"Say, 'I have a full life,'" he suggests. It's a whole different mindset. If you're living your values and doing the things you truly want, and if you're doing the work in this book, you're going to have a life full of the things that feed you and give life meaning. From the outside, it will look busy, busy, busy, but the truth is, it's just joyful.

# Pitfalls

The literal definition of pitfall is a pit in the ground, lightly covered so an animal doesn't see it until it falls in and is trapped. There's no better word for the people and activities that take you by surprise and damage the quality of your room. The following are the ones we've observed most often. If you fall into any of them, your concierge needs to get busy rearranging your room (and your doorkeeper needs to watch out for these).

## Good Intentions

We hope your heart and mind are filled with good intentions for yourself and everyone in your room. Good intent can lead you to bad commitments, however. You can love a friend and want to support them. But if that leads you to lend them money, promise a favor that is beyond your capacity, or join them in some bad behavior—such as gossiping about another friend— you will regret the place in your room that a good intention takes you.

## Noise, Drama, and Conflict

The wrong people can make your life unbearably chaotic. Have you ever felt your life was like this? Would it help if you could turn down the volume on the noise some people bring into your room? Maybe you are afraid to turn people away even when you think they might bring more disorder than help. Or you're scared or embarrassed to stop the toxic people you encounter at your door, so you let them into your room to avoid conflict, and they begin creating mass chaos.

Is your room already too full? Really loud? Full of drama? Boring? Holding angry people? Or worse yet—several of these things? Conversely, have you ever felt alone in an empty space? Lost without a road map? In need of friendship, advice, or mentoring?

We've seen this particularly within professional networks such as BNI, where people who come into a networking group can have a major impact on the success of that group. Just one wrong person can have a disastrous effect, spoiling the positive dynamic BNI groups are designed to create. If you belong to such a group, you know how quickly it can become utterly dysfunctional.

## The Bait and Switch

One day, a friend of ours was getting her hair done, and she posed this situation to her hairdresser: "I don't get it. For months I dated this guy, and he was considerate and sweet. He called me back, he appreciated me for who I am, and he was always easygoing and fun. Then we got serious. We agreed to stop seeing other people. We spent every weekend together, and I introduced him to some of my friends. Then, over the course of a few weeks, he turned into a real jerk. He doesn't call before he shows up. His language and jokes are getting mean. He seems to take me for granted. What the heck happened?"

The hairdresser summed it up beautifully, "Girl, in those first months you weren't talking to him, you were talking to his customer sales representative!"

The bait-and-switch people got into your room under false pretenses. You can give them a chance to clean up their act, but if it's clear that the customer service representative was the bait and this other person is the switch, into the lockbox and up on the shelf they go.

## Negativity

The negative person always reminds you that every silver lining has a cloud. If you get a great performance review at work, they'll say that reviews are rigged or that you'll soon be crushed by new responsibilities. Or they'll talk about the injustice of their recent performance review or how managers are all idiots—you get the idea.

Negativity might be the most common affliction we've seen in rooms. You don't have to be a rainbows-and-unicorns optimist to see that giving off lots of negativity is a way to control a relationship and dominate a room. If you find yourself regularly trying to argue the positive side of events with someone, you might consider where they belong in your room.

To be clear, we're not talking about people who are grieving a loss or dealing with depression—they deserve compassion and kindness. We are talking about people who find a kind of recreational enjoyment in anticipating the worst or spreading pessimism around the room.

There's a special case of negativity relevant to your room—the person who mocks or disdains the very idea of having a room. We learned long ago that what really matters to them is maintaining their own point of view. They'll say, "What are you talking about? The whole thing is just a metaphor!" To which we reply, "Of course it is, but like other metaphors in life, it's very personal and useful." You might ask them to consider the metaphors they use in everyday life, such as "This church is home to me" or "My team won, and I'm in heaven!"

Negativity has one thing in common with genuine depression: it is a state of mind that continually calls attention to itself. Like social media (where it thrives), negativity is typically uninterested in objective debate. We don't advise trying to convince anyone that your room is valuable; that judgment is up to you.

## Social Media, News, and Opinions

We understand you want to use social media to keep in touch with family and friends. We do that too. Many people, including us, have to use social media for business. But when we're done we move on to something else instead of "doomscrolling" for hours. The addictive qualities of social media, designed purposefully to keep people scrolling, are like other addictions: momentarily pleasurable, then requiring an ever-increasing dose to create the same buzz.

For many people, their virtual world of social media is the most chaotic and densely populated part of their room. So many of the flaming debates they have are with strangers. There's no relationship, only negative emotions shoveled at imagined adversaries or allies. Algorithms, bots, and avatars—and endless advertisements—prompt emotional reactions as well, effectively convincing users that they are interacting with real people or completing valuable activities.

Is your room full of commentators, social media figures, news figures, and celebrities? Whether they're in your room depends on how much you invest in reacting to them. This is the negative side of virtual relationships: they're like virtual mentors but with an unlimited capacity to use your time and attention. These relationships aren't real, but at their strongest, they prompt emotions that masquerade as relationships.

The treatment for addiction to social media, opinions, news, and celebrity gossip is awareness and choice. We recommend microdosing them, meaning disciplining yourself to limit your exposure to the essentials. There are so many ways to do this, they'd fill a book (in fact they have, such as Cal Newport's *A World without Email* and Adam Alter's *Irresistible*).

World crises have clarified this to us. Early in the COVID-19 pandemic, Ivan noticed folks in his virtual workshops getting caught up in the feeling that the world was coming to an end and everything was falling apart. It was a terrible time, but within the bounds of staying safe and informed, Ivan would advise people to microdose the news: "Don't sit there for hours reading the same stories and listening to the same talking heads. Everyone's routine is disrupted. See that for what it is, and contribute to hope by being empathetic, kind, and helpful. Since you have to slow down, *slow down*. You can pivot. You can contribute to a better world as we get through this. You can mourn what's lost and get busy creating the next new normal."

One of the best observations about the COVID-19 crisis came from Surgeon General Vivek Murthy, who commented that the pandemic also showed us how resilient we are and how fast we can change. He asked whether we really want to go back to 2019 or create a better, more meaningful, and more connected life as the pandemic wanes.

## Homeopathic Doses: Your Cure-All for Dealing with Difficult Loved Ones

We suspect you'd be lying if you said you don't have any loved ones whom you want to put on the highest shelf you could possibly reach—maybe even cut a hole in the ceiling and toss them in the rafters. These nuisances are often family members or longtime friends whom we love and don't want out of our lives completely. We want them in our room, but we want to take them in small doses. If only people who are best in small doses actually came in small doses!

Another way of looking at microdosing is the concept of homeopathic doses. A homeopathic dose is when you take the minutest drop of medicine to treat a problem. Arielle Ford, a leading figure in the personal growth movement, told us in an interview about the value of homeopathic doses for handling people in your room. Ford recommends creating your own guidelines for dealing with people you love but who might not align with your values or are just generally difficult to be around for whatever reason. These guidelines will help you create structure for interacting with them.

Your goal might be to see people and connect with them, but only rarely and for short periods of time. That way, you still maintain a relationship, but you don't get "infected with drama or craziness," which Ford cautions against.

Ford encourages people to make guidelines that are quickly achievable because small changes can have big effects. For instance, rather than calling someone two months in advance and telling them you'll be in town for a week, call them shortly before you arrive and ask them if they have time for a forty-five-minute get-together over tea the next day. Likewise, when your drama-addicted cousin gives you a call, tell her, "It's great to hear from you! I have only seven minutes. Let's catch up fast." You don't have to use these exact words, but you get the drift. When you use your own words, the technique can be effective.

Alternately, if you want to catch up with some friends or family members, do so at a larger gathering where you can see them and talk but where they are not your sole focus for an extended time. Holiday parties, family or class reunions, or other annual get-togethers can be perfect places to continue relationships without getting sucked into the drama.

These types of people are draining, so it's best to recognize that and plan accordingly. In other words, have a plan for managing these people so they don't elbow their way to the front of your room.

Incidentally, we like to extend the concept of homeopathic doses to activities as well. Number one on the list is social media. Another is overdosing on the 24/7 news cycle. You can convince yourself that you are just keeping yourself informed, but when you catch yourself reading political news, opinion pages, or sports news for three hours a day, you might want to move that computer or phone screen farther back in your room.

# Watch for Red Flags

There are some dead giveaways by which you can recognize candidates for the lockbox, benign neglect, or homeopathic doses. Here are the most common red flags.

## Moving the Goalposts

Some people in your room cannot be satisfied. For that matter, some of the voices in your head of people you have internalized can never be satisfied. Maybe you have a business associate who doesn't savor success but moves immediately to the next goal. There is a place for them in the world of business, but is it okay for them to move *your* goalposts as well?

The most obvious version of this pitfall is someone who changes the terms after you've agreed to them. Money and time are issues where people often fall into this trap. For example, a friend asks you to serve on a committee that they promise will take five hours a month; then you find out the amount of work you're expected to do will take you fifteen or twenty hours a month. "But you made a commitment!" they will say, to which you must answer, "I committed to five hours a month, and I'm doing that cheerfully. But your need for more time doesn't change my capacity to give it to you."

There's also a special version of overdoing it, which we call *reverse perfectionism*. That's the voice that says, after you've hit a goal, "Well, that wasn't so great." Sometimes it comes as an urge to compare yourself to an impossible ideal, such as dwelling on the fact that you will never be as good a physicist as Albert Einstein, as brilliant an entrepreneur as Steve Jobs, or as famous as your favorite celebrity. When you hear this voice, write down what it says, and ask, Am I moving the goalposts on myself? Who in your room taught you to do that?

## Going to Extremes

One well-disguised pitfall of your room is extreme thinking. If you say, "That's it—I'll never let another [fill in the blank] into my room again!" or conversely "Anyone like [fill in the blank] is welcome to be in my room up close and personal forever!" you are eventually going to make a serious mistake. You'll let someone in because they *appear* right or keep someone out because they *appear* wrong rather than finding out enough about them to make a reasoned decision.

You are going to make mistakes because you're human. That's why you have a doorkeeper and a concierge who empower you to correct your mistakes. That said, you can tell some forms of extreme behavior long before you let someone in or allow them to get close. Here are a few examples:

*People who say "You always . . ." or "You never . . ."*—These people want to reduce your behavior to a cartoon character of yourself. The Road Runner always gets away; Wile E. Coyote never catches him. In real life, always and never are very rare.

*Catastrophizing people*—These people behave as if every setback is a catastrophe or expand every mistake into a life-threatening situation. We have sympathy for these people because typically they have lost a sense of proportion due to some past trauma. For example, a person who grew up with a physically abusive parent might feel that every disagreement is tantamount to a beating. Someone who grew up in poverty might feel an exaggerated sense of impending financial ruin far exceeding reality. Treat them gently and let them know that, for the sake of a healthy relationship, they need to differentiate between a little trouble and real disaster.

*Minimizing people*—These people are the opposite of catastrophizing people. These folks see life's difficulties as no big deal as long as they happen to someone else. They say, "If you'd just . . ." a lot, as in "If you'd just change jobs, everything would be fine." Most of life is more complicated than that. Be cautious about taking their minimizing to heart; your concierge might need to set boundaries on their simplistic prescriptions.

These and other forms of black-and-white, no-middle-ground, all-or-nothing extremes might be motivating for a few people (Olympic athletes come to mind). We don't dispute their right to run their lives at the far end of reason, but they don't have the right to impose their personal standards on you or your room.

# Don't Wait to Speak Your Truth: Joanie's Story Part II

*Stewart's wife, Joanie Emery, shared this story about speaking the truth to family.*

When I was little, I would sit on my dad's lap and read. When I make a mistake, he told me I was stupid. And at one point, he threw me across the room. It broke my heart, and it got me to shut down. As a child, I did everything I could to be a good daughter. I made sure everybody liked me, I said and did the right things, but I did it all at my own cost.

About twenty years later, after I'd been doing a lot of Who's In Your Room? work, I visited my parents in Colorado. My dad asked me to go for a hike, and I said to Stewart, "I can't go on a walk with my dad. I have nothing to say to him. It's going to be horrible." But Stewart said, "The worst thing you could do is not talk to him."

So my dad and I went hiking, and at one point I said, "Can I talk to you about something?" And he said yes. I described what he had done when I was young and said, "That hurt me beyond belief. When you treated me as if I wasn't worth anything, it shattered me."

And he looked at me and he said, "Joanie, I am so sorry. I never would intentionally do anything to hurt you. It's all I knew how to do because that's the way my dad related to me."

That single conversation had a big impact on my relationship with my dad. It started a healing process with us. He went from walking out of a room when I came in to telling me, "I love you," whenever we were on the phone and saying, "When are you coming?" and "Please don't leave." That was the beginning of a whole new experience with him for me.

I realized that if I had only said something earlier, we might have had that conversation years ago, and I might have avoided a lot of pain and suffering. I also realized that it was not too late, and after that conversation, we had so many years of joy and laughter.

## Your Joys and Pitfalls Timeline

If any of these joys and pitfalls resonate for you, take some time to list them and write about how they have affected the quality of your room. We suggest a different form for this list—a timeline. Write the years since your childhood in a descending column on the left side of a page. You can group them together with labels like "school years" and "first jobs" or list each year. Next to these years, write a joy, a pitfall, or both and a sentence or two about what happened and why. As you go, you will see patterns about whom you let into your room that had a positive or negative effect. How did they influence you? It could be teachers, parents, siblings, your first romantic interest or partner, figures of authority, or people such as bosses who had influence over your well-being. The point here is to see how you have internalized the behaviors, beliefs, and attitudes of others—how everybody who's been in your room still affects you.

Table 2 shows a short example.

TABLE 2. Timeline Example

| Years | Joy | Pitfall |
|---|---|---|
| College | • Prof. Reynolds: mentor who inspired me to love music<br>• Discovering jazz; collaborating with Derek, Tempe, Bill, and Chicky | • Overcommitting to my sorority<br>• Accepting Sean's need to judge me harshly |
| First job | • Earning a paycheck—feeling independence | • People-pleasing (constant)<br>• Lots of drama with peers |
| Moved to Chicago | • Being far away from home—more independence, up to me<br>• New friends like Amanda | • Impulsively choosing the wrong roommates<br>• Postponing the decision to move out for too long |

## You're in My Room but Your Project Isn't: Stewart's Story

*Stewart tells this story of responding to a friend's request with compassion while still setting limits. The happy outcome surprised him.*

Melissa is a dear friend. In fact, if Joan and I had been blessed with a daughter, and if she had turned out just like Melissa, I would've been thrilled. But now there was a problem. Melissa was trying to persuade me to do a startup with her.

Melissa is an exceptionally talented executive coach. In fact, she's so good that she coaches senior people in a number of the world's most prestigious consulting firms. She had observed that many folks travel through life blissfully unaware of how other people experience them. She believes that if people are going to have a shot at enduring success and happiness in life, they need to proceed from a place that includes self-awareness. She had dreamed up an idea for a web-based business that would give people the opportunity to have a personality portrait of themselves painted for them by others who had known them over the years of their life.

I had tried a number of gentle ways to say I couldn't be involved. My first approach was to simply say that at my age I was way beyond another startup. Melissa, being the great coach that she is, pointed out that I had built a career based in part on helping people reinvent themselves and by letting them know that it was never too late and that therefore I could do this startup with her. Several other strategies didn't work any better. And then I heard about this idea of the room. I texted Melissa an invitation to meet for coffee.

We met at Peet's Coffee. I ordered a double espresso and currant scone; Melissa ordered organic herbal tea. I told her the story of how I learned about the doorkeeper idea and this question "Who's in your room?" Then I moved into what I thought would be the brilliant part. I told her that I loved her like a daughter and that she would always be in my room. But her startup was not in my room and never would be. Melissa started crying—not loudly enough for other patrons to turn and stare but visibly enough to get my full attention.

As a man, I have at last learned that anything I might say next in an attempt to fix things is bound not to help. Obviously what I had thought would be the brilliant part wasn't, so I did my best to stay parked in neutral and wait for what was coming next. Next was a surprise.

Through the gentlest of tears and the sweetest of smiles, Melissa explained to me that it had never been about the startup. All she wanted was to be in my room as a dear friend and that she had believed she would never be invited in if she didn't knock on the door with a project in hand.

I just love happy endings. I could also see that my Door-keeper needed further training to better understand what it was that people really wanted when they came knocking on the door of my room.

Your doorkeeper, concierge, and all that goes in your room need tweaking and adjusting from time to time. Remember, this is a tailor-made arrangement, and, just like the clothes you wear, sometimes it needs to be let out a bit or taken in some. Life is short, and there are just so many breaths in it, so focusing on your values also has to do with how much you can enjoy and savor life.

# 9

# When Bad Things Happen in Good Rooms

LIFE IS NOT perfect. You might have noticed that.

Recognizing that people can never fully leave your room once they've entered can be unsettling. What do we do with all the people who don't align with our values or the people we misjudged? Some people in your room might have changed for the worse. And let's face it: What about family? And longtime friends? How do we handle them? As you've worked through this book, those questions have probably been playing somewhere in the back (or front) of your mind.

You have to tame this elephant in your room because even when you *think* people are out of your life, they remain in your head. You need a management strategy for difficult people. We've suggested your concierge can escort them to the lockbox and put them on the shelf. However, we know that even if you like this idea, there are a few people in your life about whom you say, "Yeah, but . . ." *But* I see them at holidays. *But* she's my boss. *But* I owe him money. *But* they're my brother's partner, and I love my brother. *But* no matter how obnoxious he is, he's my brother. And so on.

This chapter is about externalities—the people who entered your room before you thought about keeping them out and the people who try to force their way into your room now to leverage a connection of some kind. It's natural to feel some hesitation about dealing with any of them, but as you become clearer about who's in your room, you become more invested in moving the toxic people away and the beneficial people closer.

## Start with Your Family

Some people are blessed with perfect families. They have no challenges or conflicts among family members, and everybody gets along from childhood to old age.

Yeah, we don't know any of those families either.

For the rest of us, family are the first people in our rooms. By *family* we mean all kinds of families—birth families, adoptive families, extended families. The child raised in a mountain monastery has a family of monks or nuns. The middle child of a dilettante billionaire has a family of stepsiblings. In any form, these people are the first in our rooms. They have a customary claim to their place.

While they have a prerogative to be in your room, *you* decide their location—close, far, or in the lockbox and on the shelf. You also decide how the choices they make affect your relationship. The saying "You can choose your friends, you can choose your partner, but you can't choose your family" needs to extend outward. You can't choose your partner's family either (cue the in-law jokes), but you can decide where they belong and under what conditions.

Family is the place where boundaries are a flash point because you have a set of people who typically grew up with the same expectations, and anyone who changes those expectations can and will be challenged. Do you have space for disagreements? Do you know how to set boundaries that are different from the ones you learned as a child?

According to the family systems theory in psychology, individuals are viewed as participants in a complex system of emotional demands, expectations, loyalty, belief systems (such as culture and religion), shared history, and various coalitions (we're simplifying here). As members of the system differentiate themselves through adolescence and adulthood, others react. Sometimes they perpetuate a familiar state. For example, a family that grows up perpetually in crisis might react to a member stepping away from the drama by ratcheting it up or forcing a crisis.

If you decide that a family member is too close in your room and then you set boundaries on their behavior, don't expect them to instantly change or even agree you have a valid point. Whatever their reaction, consider whether they are trying to maintain the system you once shared because you are disturbing that system. Consider also that by managing your room, you are differentiating yourself from your earlier role of boss, caretaker, peacemaker, loser, "Dad's favorite," or whatever label was put on you in the past.

How do family members know where your buttons are and how to push them? Easy—they installed them long ago. You were assigned a role and either cooperated with it or reacted against it. Families create a shared narrative that wants people to stay in their roles. People invested in the family status quo push those buttons to keep everyone in their place. You have to be alert for those buttons, whether they're accusations of guilt, disloyalty, or something else. No matter how hard others push, move firmly through the process of setting limits.

This is the painful part of working with your room: the realization that you need to change somebody's place in your room, followed by a difficult middle period of adjusting, leading to the feeling of relief and liberation when they are in the right place. Families, with their long-standing loyalties and issues, can make that middle period especially hard.

This need not be a big fight if you approach the moment with a spirit of making life better for yourself and the people you love. You might explain the concept of the room and describe the work you've done as making you more available and authentic. You might share your own difficulty in breaking out of the family system by rearranging your room. It's also fine to sincerely say, "I love you, and I will always be your brother/sister/son/daughter/etc. I need to do this to be available to you, even in small doses."

Working with family members in your room isn't always negative. We encourage you to consider who should be closer to you and why they are not. Right now, you might be considering that sister you call only once a year just because she was much older and you haven't lived in the same state since she went to college. If she belongs closer in your room, you have the power to change the inertia of habit and get in touch more often. Perhaps you can find opportunities to show an interest in her partner or children; when you deliberately bring someone closer, you can be open to life-enhancing, revived relationships.

Are you feeling a sense of dread when you imagine the actions you might take to improve your family relationships? Is there something in you right now saying, "Oh, I can't talk about that!" We have good news—the work of your room is the work of a lifetime. Don't expect instant change in yourself or others. If you and your concierge move in the direction of love—for your family and yourself—new opportunities will appear.

Your room is not a movie script in which every loose end is tied up at the end of two hours. If you want to bring a family member closer, try taking one small action to improve your relationship. If you want to start small, it's not mandatory to describe the Who's in Your Room? framework. Maybe you can invite that distant sister to a virtual coffee or cocktail hour and just spend time listening to them. Maybe their children and yours, cousins who have never met, can find a way to see each other next summer. Even just picking up the phone to ask "How are you?" is a good start.

This kind of loving act is the positive opposite of setting boundaries. Let's call it making space for them to come a little closer if they want to.

## Rules of the Room

Sometimes families use a common mechanism to preserve the system: triangulation. That's when person A has a problem with person B but won't deal directly with them, so they drag person C into the matter. You see it in exchanges such as "Hey, you're closer to Johnny than I am. Would you talk to him about his drinking?" "Mom's never been fair about money, especially to me, but don't tell her I said so," and "Why does Marianne seem so hostile to my partner?"

Triangulation is the tool of people who don't want to face a problem in a relationship head on because they're uncomfortable, afraid, or maintaining a façade. It's rarely helpful and typically causes resentment in person C, even if they want to help.

The boundary you need to set on triangulation is simple: don't engage in it. Instead, tell the person asking that they need to deal directly with the third person. If it won't violate your own boundaries, you might offer to be present when a direct conversation takes place. But add your perspective in an impartial way.

Sometimes a person observes a problem between two family members and offers to help because they are skilled at bringing people together in an impartial way. That's mediation, not triangulation. But if the problem is serious, find someone detached from the family drama—a therapist, financial advisor, or doctor—to help with the issue.

---

# An Ex-Spouse Learns to Rule Her Room

*A person can be so used to their family system that they don't even notice what's going on. A close friend described how his former spouse finally realized the cost of a toxic family and what happened when she took action.*

My ex-wife was living in the Northeast after we divorced; she was miserable, partly because she had people in her room that she did not need. Her parents were irrational about family issues and treated her poorly. Their pain makes them happy, or at least *think* they're happy. And her sister—how shall I put this succinctly—is as close to a psychopath as I ever hope to meet.

One day I was returning with my daughter from a family gathering up north. Both she and my son had moved to Texas for school. My girl was quiet for a long time, and then she said, "Daddy, I know I'm only about twenty years old, but I've never met anyone like Aunt Irene. She has no redeeming characteristics whatsoever."

When a twenty-year-old nails the situation like that, you have to do something. I called my ex (with whom I have a great friendship) and said, "There are three people in your room who are making you absolutely miserable. They are so deep in your room, and so close to you, that they are ruining your life. Their names are Mom, Dad, and Irene." Then I explained the room concept, the doorkeeper, the concierge, and the lockbox.

A little time passed. My ex moved to Texas, near to the people that, however imperfect, belong up close in her room—namely our daughter and son. About a year after that, she helped my daughter move into a new place. They spent seven days together and had a great time. My daughter was amazed. She said, "Dad, I spent a week with Mom, and she didn't drive me crazy like she always does."

I said, "Honey, there's a reason for that." And I explained to her the concept of the room. I said, "Your mother now has a baseline of happiness that she never had up north that allows her the space to feel and behave differently. Her head is clear, and her room is positive, with all the toxic people in their rightful places. As a consequence, she can experience an outlook of abundance instead of starving for positive interaction. She rearranged her room so the right people are up close and the others are far away."

There's an expression for the ex-wife's actions: *the geographical cure*. It doesn't work if you're running away from yourself, but it can be helpful when proximity to certain people makes you miserable. We're not recommending as dramatic a step as moving eighteen hundred miles, but sometimes that's what it takes.

## The Spirits in My Room: Doug's Story

*Even if people are no longer in this world, they are still in your room. Doug shares how he continues his relationships with those long gone.*

Whenever I enter a cathedral, I go to the bank of candles near the entrance, drop a coin into the offering box, and light a candle. I slowly say a few prayers for the people in my room who are no longer living.

I am not a Catholic, and I certainly mean no disrespect to the church. I'm not hedging my bets about the cosmos. Instead, I am grateful for the opportunity offered by that particular arrangement in all the great cathedrals of Europe and many churches elsewhere to remind myself that I am surrounded by spirits real or imagined. I don't have to be certain about the existence of a soul to appreciate their continuing presence in my life and thus in my room.

I am taking the opportunity to remind myself that even though someone has died, they are emphatically somewhere in my room. I do this periodically in my home as well. I light a candle and thank certain people for the gifts they gave me. I ask for forgiveness for mistakes I made with them and tell them that I forgive their mistakes. I say I love them, and I say I now let them go to wherever we go when we're gone. But as long as I'm in this world, they're in my room.

There's my long-ago girlfriend Joan, who got sober after we broke up, found a job at a press specializing in publishing for disabled people, and died much too young of cancer. There's JD, the best man at my wedding and as bighearted a friend as you would ever want to meet. He toppled over one morning on his way to the airport and never woke up. There's my father, my role model and hero, who disappeared into Alzheimer's long before his body gave up. And my mother, who was funny and smart and, like my father, served in the American armed forces in World War II. There are many others who I sometimes call, in the words of Dylan Thomas, all "my dead dears."

Their proximity in my room depends on the relationship we had, and still have, because of the positive things they brought into my life. My mother's best friend Louise, a very successful businesswoman in the 1950s (when that was quite rare), taught me, "When you're feeling sorry for yourself, go help someone!" My onetime boss Jack, a gruff magazine editor, taught me at least a dozen expressions so colorful that I still use them today (a favorite is "That man's tougher than Dogleg Chewing Tobacco"). My church friend Gene announced every year at the annual meeting that "if you're a member of this community, you must add in your time, talents, and treasure."

I have a concierge who keeps the spirits in my room a little ways away, not in my innermost circle but available to come close when I need perspective. They offer me the lives they lived and remind me that I must make the most of the breaths I have left.

## Spring Cleaning

Your room needs periodic cleaning and disinfecting. That means removing some of the toxic waste that people have brought in with them: debts, conflicting values, attitudes, and especially whatever baggage they decided to drop off. They might be way over in their lockbox on the shelf, but their footprints left a big mess.

One immutable law of nature is that everything is changing and in motion all the time. Cosmologists can explain the science of this, but we prefer a simpler example: every building starts the process of falling apart from the moment it's completed. Sooner or later the furnace is going to go or the roof needs replacing or the foundation cracks. That's just inherent in the nature of a building. Your room is also constantly changing, obeying the laws of inertia and powers of gravity, however, metaphorically so. That means your doorkeeper and concierge can never retire. They are ready at any time to decide whether someone can enter your room and where they should go.

Your room has changed a lot since you were a teenager. Of course, your doorkeeper let in a lot more people, and over the years these people came closer or went farther away from you. Change is inevitable; you cannot stop it, but you can make a conscious effort to direct it. That's what we mean by giving your room a periodic cleaning.

We wrote a lot about family because they have a great impact on your life. Here are three examples of other people who can make bad things happen in good rooms:

- *Bad bosses*—We mentioned these antimentors earlier, and they merit repeating because, face it, we've all had them. Many were simply incompetent, clueless, or both, like the boss in *Dilbert*. Others were actively malevolent, playing out their particular obsessions—money, power, advancement—regardless of whom they damaged. Others were just replaying their family system in the workplace. Writer Joe Pinsker observed that when companies say, "We're like family here," it can mean "We'll foist obligations upon you, expect your unconditional devotion, disrespect your boundaries, and be bitter if you prioritize something above us."

- *Fakes*—Some people feign friendship or interest but quickly reveal that their only interest is exploiting your connections, selling you something, or enlisting you in their cause. Business and networking groups and online platforms are often abused by these people—which is why Ivan designed BNI with protocols to prevent them from infiltrating a group and keep them out of authentic members' rooms.
- *Toxic neighbors*—This is a tough one to handle because they are in physical proximity, and unless they violate the law, there's little you can do. One of us tried for years to deal with a toxic neighbor, finally building a high fence. The neighbor did not improve, but that act of moving them to the far end of the room improved the situation.

You can think of others specific to your room. Once again, you can return to the list of who's in your room that you created in chapter 3, remind yourself of their presence, and tell your concierge what to do with them.

## Adversaries Are Your Teachers

The Stoics in Greek classical times spoke brilliantly about life's difficulties. To oversimplify one of their key insights, it's not the things that happen to you that matter, it's your point of view about those things. The externalities are not under your control, but how you react to them can bring you to despair or liberation. You'll find similar sentiments in Buddhist teachings, in other ancient religions and philosophies, and in modern works like Viktor Frankl's *Man's Search for Meaning*.

You'll even find this point of view in Shakespeare's plays, such as Hamlet's remark that "There is nothing either good or bad, but thinking makes it so" and Duke Senior's observation that "Sweet are the uses of adversity."

It's precisely because nobody leaves your room that you have such a rich opportunity to reflect on how your own reaction to them commands your actions. When you meet a difficulty and instantly think, "Poor me," consider how you might react differently. You might discover that your worst adversaries are your best teachers.

## The Costliest People in Your Room

By now your notebook has a lot of names and descriptions of the positive and negative people in your room. If you haven't already, look at both and prioritize the lists from the most to least extreme examples. Again, write in depth what you know about them, your relationship to them, and where they belong in your room. A provocative way to do this exercise is to alternate between the extremes: With whom do you have the worst relationship in your family? How about the best? How does each operate within the family system? You might be surprised, for example, to find that they are both operating in the same system but with completely different attitudes or perspectives. What does that tell you?

Try the same with work or business: list the worst relationship and the best. In what ways are they similar? Are they far apart in your room or equally close? How can you set boundaries with one and invite the other to come closer?

# Everyone in Your Room Is Your Teacher: Cynthia's Story

*Cynthia James is a strong-willed African American woman who transcended a childhood of violence and abuse to acquire two master's degrees, serve as a minister and missionary, and author such books as* What Will Set You Free—*used in workshops for women in prisons—*Revealing Your Extraordinary Essence, *and* I Choose Me.

When I first heard the concept of Who's in Your Room? I knew that I had to pay attention. My whole body reverberated. I started going through my inner files and thought of many people whom I loved who were in my room, and many whom, in retrospect, I would not have invited in if I had been awake. Then a small thought entered: "They were all your teachers." That was followed by a more powerful thought: "Did you really have to learn so many hard lessons?" Wow! What a concept. I could have invited the kind of teachers into my room who didn't need to evoke drama, betrayal, pain, and suffering.

Let me back up for a moment. I was born into a childhood that was far from nurturing. There was a lot of violence, confusion, struggle, and crisis. It seemed natural because my grandmother, mother, aunts, uncles, and cousins were all living the same sort of life. It never dawned on me that there could be something else, alternatives. My early school years were filled with emotional explosions of one kind or another. We moved a lot when I was a child, and it was difficult to make friends.

My first real friend whom I remember was Vernice. She lived next door, and we would visit each other often. I was desperate to have a friend, so I accepted any treatment she was willing to offer. I wanted to be in her room in the worst way.

Many times she was mean, condescending, and downright cruel. One day, she became angry with me at school. We lived in Minnesota, where winters are harsh. It was below zero that day. Vernice took my coat and ran home, leaving me to walk almost a mile in the cold. When I got home, I was half frozen and deeply angry.

I walked to her door and knocked. She opened it, and I punched her in the nose with all my strength. Her nose started bleeding, and she ran into her house screaming. I walked away feeling proud of myself for standing up. As I think about this incident today, it is how I lived much of my life. I would invite people in, allow them to treat me in challenging ways, and then at some point get fed up and create some intense experience.

The abuse and trauma in my life planted seeds within me of low self-esteem, doubt, and fear-based thinking. Vernice was only one example of people that I invited into my life out of desperation. I had an intense need to be loved, seen, heard, and acknowledged. I kept looking for and attracting people who treated me badly. The interesting thing about this is that everyone I chose mirrored my childhood. Well into my twenties, I began to realize that my life wasn't working. I knew that I was somehow involved in the dysfunction, but I didn't have a clue how to change it, so I kept stumbling along until one day I found myself in a personal-development workshop.

The leader said, "Everything that is in your life is a reflection of what you believe you deserve." I was stunned. How could that be? How could I possibly believe I deserved to be betrayed, dishonored, and manipulated? He had to be wrong. At the end of the workshop, I approached the facilitator and shared my disbelief. He was kind and said, "Was your childhood a challenge?" I said, "Yes." He looked at me and said, "Perhaps, your childhood taught you to expect bad things, and your family members were unconscious teachers." My body tingled with goose bumps, and I knew there was truth in what he was saying. That moment began a great journey of self-discovery and a quiet determination to heal these old wounds. I committed to learning to love myself and create a life that I could only dream of as a child.

I would love to tell you that this was an easy journey and that my life instantly shifted once I had the revelation. However, nothing could be further from the truth. It took years of therapy, seminars, spiritual explorations, and creating more interesting experiences. I continued to kiss frogs, hoping they were princes. I continued to put myself in situations where I felt used and misunderstood. I continued to blame others for my life's challenges.

The good news is that somewhere along the line, I actually woke up. I began to see that no one was doing anything to me. These painful experiences were the result of my inviting people into my life and never asking for what I truly needed. I began to awaken sooner each time and recognize how these people and events were, indeed, mirroring back to me how I perceived myself and how I believed I deserved to be treated. I began to understand that it was possible to say no, that I could choose how I wanted to live. I became aware that many times I was treating myself in the same ways that I accused others of treating me.

Although I would not wish my childhood pain on anyone, many of the experiences and lessons have supported me in doing the work that I do today with people and organizations. At this point in my life, I am intentional about who is invited into my world. Once people come into your room, they are there with you forever. All the people that have crossed my path are still with me. Some of them are physically still in my life. We have grown together and supported each other to become more conscious beings. Others have moved away to reveal their own life lessons. And still others I left or asked them to leave since I had outgrown my need for dysfunctional relationships.

I don't believe that old relationships have to come forward to test us. However, I do believe these relationships live within us and remind us of what we have chosen. Their presence in our lives and our memories influence how we currently choose to live.

Today, I am extraordinarily grateful for my life and treasure each moment. I have learned to listen to my intuition and trust my instincts. My current room is alive and active. It is filled with people who are dedicated to growth, committed to being change agents, and consciously love themselves and others. I have a loving husband and have created healthy relationships. We do not always agree, but respect is present and trust is ever expanding. I have a gratitude chamber for the people and circumstances that once served me but are no longer necessary. It is a lovely little space where they can be comfortable. But make no mistake about it. The room is locked, and I hold the key next to my heart.

There is nothing more quiet and personal than your room when it is functioning well and in balance. Often this happens because you've faced the bad things that are happening or have happened in your room. Cynthia is an inspiring example of how intentionality, self-awareness, self-honesty, and lifelong persistence steadily create a better and better room.

# 10

# Live in Your Flame, Not in Your Wax

THE POWER of the Who's in Your Room? framework is that by working with these ideas and making them your own, you focus on bringing people and ideas into your room to support the future you desire. The concepts of the doorkeeper and the concierge are simple but powerful reminders that you make decisions every day about where you will put your attention. What will you do, as our friend Geneen asks, with the breaths you have left?

You can give away your power to people who are in your room but don't have your best interests in mind—the people who don't share your values or appreciate your right to decide for yourself what you will be, whom you will love, or how you will behave. This usually happens in small, incremental steps— giving away a bit of your integrity for approval, money, or power of some kind.

Or you can choose a life of integrity and mutuality. You can bring people close to you who can benefit from what you have to give, whether that is love, a job, valuable advice, or money. You can gently (or not so gently) put the toxic people in the lockbox and on the shelf and create more space for the people who feed your mind, heart, and soul.

You don't have to surround yourself with people who agree with you all the time. Sometimes the richest relationships happen between people of very different backgrounds or viewpoints. The relationships work because they are based on mutual respect and friendship. You also don't have to agree with us on every point, but we have written this book and spoken about the room to thousands of people because we respect their right to choose for themselves.

This book, with its simple metaphor of the room, is about taking your power back. It's also about being accountable for your decisions and honoring your values. It's about creating more space for the positive and less for the negative.

The following story illustrates our point: One day, a young American intellectual visited a wisdom master in Asia. He asked the master questions about the nature of reality and the mind, and with each new question, he spoke about all the ideas he had studied and knew on the subject. The master listened patiently for several hours and then said, "Let's have tea."

A servant brought in a beautiful tea service, and the master set a cup before the student. He poured tea until the cup was full. Then he kept pouring. Tea spilled over the brim and onto the table. The master kept pouring.

The student jumped up and exclaimed, "Stop, stop! Can't you see the cup is full? All that tea is wasted!"

The master replied, "Yes, and your mind is also full. You will have to empty it first."

That's what we mean by creating space. Your metaphorical room might be infinite, but your life on earth is not. Since nobody can leave the room, you will be banishing the unwanted elements to the lockbox on the shelf to create space for the existing and new relationships that will feed you.

## Live in Your Flame

When Ivan speaks before a BNI event or other gathering, he is often asked to spell out simple ways to improve one's life. He shares the story of the room, of course, and also the fallacy of balance (see below). And then he asks people to "live in your flame, not in your wax." People always understand where they are in their lives—flame or wax.

When you're living in your flame, you're excited. You're doing the things that you absolutely love. People can hear it in your voice and see it in the way you behave.

We urge you to create a room where you're able to live in your flame. You need to be doing the things that bring you joy and excitement and that you're passionate about. You need to surround yourself with people who are receptive to that flame and also on fire. That's what it means to live in your flame.

You also know when you're living in your wax. You say, "I gotta get up and go to work. I hate what I'm doing. Life is a drag. The people I have to deal with are taking the energy out of my life." It's easy to surround yourself with other wax makers. You're all working in your wax, and you all hate it and complain about it. But nothing will change until that wax gets burned up in the heat of your own passion, beliefs, and love.

Ivan illustrates how simple that wax can be: Early on in his business, he realized that one element of his wax was accounting. He hated accounting. He could get around a financial statement, but he just didn't like it, so one of the first positions he hired was a bookkeeper. She said accounting was her flame.

One day the bookkeeper came to Ivan and said, "The books didn't balance." Ivan thought this would cause trouble, until she said, "They're off by five cents."

It took her two hours, but she found those five pennies. A friend asked Ivan if he reprimanded her for wasting so much time. Ivan said, "Are you kidding? This is the perfect person for that job! Five pennies and she's chasing them down because that's her flame!"

Early in your life and in your work, you can't live in your flame all the time. That's why it's important to reinvent yourself. Ivan started as a management consultant and became an entrepreneur, going from solopreneur to running an international company. Stewart has created multiple businesses, been a consultant to huge corporations, written books, and created some of the world's most successful marketing campaigns. Doug went from book publishing to magazines to a top-fifty internet business and reinvented himself as a full-time writer at age forty-six.

Over time, you learn to live more in your flame than in your wax, and managing your room is an indispensable way to move in that direction. You create space to focus on the activities that bring mastery and fulfillment. You will have time to practice.

The great cellist Pablo Casals was asked in his seventies why he continued to practice four or more hours a day. He replied, "Because I think I am making progress."

## Happiness and Fulfillment

We have spoken and written about happiness and fulfillment for years, and what we have found is this: people who say happiness is a human's natural state are mistaken. It was a popular proposal in the human potential movement and still gains currency in the media. But evolutionary biologists point out that negative feelings are more motivating than positive feelings. They might be physical, such as hunger or cold. They might be emotional, such as fear. They might be spiritual, such as the Buddhist term *dukkha*, often translated as suffering but more accurately described as a sense of unsatisfactoriness. Put another way, humans (and other creatures) are genetically engineered to improve their situation. We seek food when we are hungry, warmth when we are cold, safety when we are frightened.

And happiness? We seek that, too, but the nature of happiness is that it is fleeting. Soon another desire will arise, and we will feel discontent and seek contentment again. There's nothing inherently wrong with chasing after happiness; the problem with most people is that they think of it as a permanent state.

The state we encourage you to seek is fulfillment. Make the best possible use you can of your skills, values, actions, circumstances, beliefs—the whole package. Use yourself up in your flame. You will find fulfillment, and also a source of happiness.

## In My Son's Room: Ivan's Story
## Part II

*Building a life of harmony includes paying attention to the most important relationships in your room, and that's not just a matter of spending time with people. The way you spend your time with someone—your attention and interest in their happiness—matters more than the sum total of hours.*

I have 2.3 million frequent-flyer miles on one airline, the equivalent of about five round trips to the moon. That means I traveled a *lot* as my kids were growing up. I didn't have much balance between work and home, but I tried to have a life of harmony, to make the things I care about, including work and family, matter equally.

One day when my son was seventeen, we were sitting in front of a big-screen television playing a game of *Halo*. Suddenly I asked, "Hey, was I around enough for you as you were growing up?"

My son looked up from the screen and said, "You were around all the time!'"

I said, "I don't know if you noticed, buddy, but I'm gone about every other week for at least three or four days, sometimes a week."

He said, "Yeah, yeah, I know. I know." Then he added, "I don't know if you noticed, but when you're here, you're *really* here. Can we get back to the game now?"

That's how to be in someone else's room.

## Seek Harmony, Not Balance

If you're like most people, at some point in time—possibly even today—you've thought about having better balance in your life. In this crazy, hectic, technology-driven society, balance is an ever-present concern for many people.

Would you like to learn the secret to balance? Here it is: forget about balance; it's an illusion. Balance assumes that we spend an *equal* amount of time in all or most areas of our life. It is like the image of the scales of justice where everything is completely in balance and equal. The concept of balance implies that we must spend a certain portion of each week devoted in some equal measure to every item important in our life.

The problem with this is that most people can't achieve this on a regular basis. We tend to live such hectic, busy lives that it is incredibly difficult to fit it all in.

But there's good news. We suggest striving for *harmony*, not balance, as you live in your room.

This is more than semantics—it is a different way of looking at life. While life can't be fully in balance, it is possible to create a life that is in harmony with your values and vision of who you are and what you want to do. Even yin and yang, expressed as a familiar symbol of harmony (see figure 2), are out of balance if you look at each piece separately. If you were to pull the teardrop-shaped halves apart, they would tip over, out of balance.

FIGURE 2. Yin and yang

But together they achieve harmony. The key to this understanding is to stop stressing over whether you have perfect balance and instead become more deliberate in the choices you
make, managing your capacity for work, play, family, and everything else you want for a full life.

Psychologists and therapists largely agree that awareness is
curative. In this vein, we believe you likely won't be able to have
harmony in your room if you aren't aware of the people and
activities that bring you deep satisfaction.

To bring harmony to your room, find a place where you can sit in silence for a while. Have a pen and paper handy. You may find it helpful to gently close your eyes and focus your awareness on the process of your breathing for a while. Then begin to review the moments throughout your life when you felt most alive—when you were living in your flame.

Ask yourself the following questions:

- What am I doing when I feel most alive? Whom am I with?
- When am I enjoying myself so much that I lose track of time?
- What do I look forward to doing the most?
- What makes me feel fulfilled and satisfied?
- When have I felt the proudest? Was I alone or with someone?

The goal here is simple: identify the people, activities, and projects in your life that make you feel alive, satisfied, or fulfilled.

To take this exercise a step further, you can also write a paragraph about each activity that gives you a sense of aliveness. What does that look like? Describe each activity as vividly as possible, and take some time to think through what it would look like to experience each activity more fully and frequently. You might be surprised by what you discover. As a friend of ours started managing her room, she realized that it wasn't fancy dates with business executives who took her on helicopter and plane rides to exotic places that made her feel most alive; rather it was the deep and meaningful relationship with a firefighter, who is now her husband. It wasn't about the glamour; it was about the relationship.

# Living in Harmony

In addition to being intentional about whom you let into your room, here are some techniques that we've developed to help us—and you—live in a room full of harmony. The power of these simple strategies will change your room and your life, but you must take action to make them happen. Write them down and refer to them daily until they are a part of your routine. We've mentioned some of these in various parts of the book, and this is a short list of the best practices.

### Be Here Now

These three simple words "be here now" will make a huge difference in creating harmony in your life. *Wherever you are, be there.* If you are at work, don't be thinking about the time you didn't spend with your family the night before or what you should be doing with your spouse or partner. When you are at home, don't be thinking about the work you have to do at the office. Wherever you are, be there fully and completely. This profound truth is worth studying; many books are entirely devoted to the subject.

### Manage Your Time Creatively

If you have a big project at work that has to be done and you want to spend time with your family in the evening, get creative. We know someone who wrote his first book while his family slept. He would spend time with them in the evenings, and after everyone was asleep, he wrote and ultimately finished the book without taking any time away from his family. We know parents who are pros at switching from parenting mode to work mode the minute their child takes a nap. Be creative and inventive in finding ways that you can accomplish what you need to do yet still allow you to spend time with the precious people in your life who bring you harmony. And remember, many tasks and projects have a finite timeline. You won't always have to resort to this type of creativity unless you want to.

## Integrate Elements of Your Life

For many years, Ivan spent a couple weeks or more working remotely from his lake house in the mountains. During that time, he worked his normal hours but also had quality time with his family in a vacation setting. Sometimes he would have his staff and management team up for short retreats and workdays. It was a great way to integrate work life into a leisure environment. During the last week or so of his stay at the lake house, he exclusively spent time with his family and didn't think about work.

Note that we aren't saying you should work during all your vacations. What we're suggesting is there may be times when it makes sense to consciously integrate activities so you can have more harmony in your room. Look for ways to combine elements of your life whenever possible and practical, and do it in a conscious way.

## Practice Letting Go and Holding On

Contrary to popular belief, we do not think it is possible to have it all. Unfortunately, life involves making choices. Practice understanding what things to say no to and then letting go of them. At the same time, think about what is truly important in your life, and hold on to it with all your might.

## Create Margins

Life for people in this day and age is incredibly busy. People will take up every spare moment in your life if you let them, so it is important to create a life that has margins. Build free time, family time, and personal time into the margins of your day-to-day existence. We know someone who has wine o'clock each evening with his wife, when they enjoy a glass of wine, sit on the porch, talk about their day, and watch nature. No matter what this margin is, if you don't schedule it, it won't happen. You won't make it to the gym if it's not on your calendar. You'll be happier when you create margins, we promise. Schedule time to relax.

## Enforce Boundaries

We bet you don't enforce the boundaries you desire in life. Worse yet, we're almost certain that you don't often communicate those boundaries to others. You need your doorkeeper and concierge to communicate your boundaries to the people in your room and then guard them jealously. Don't make apologies for the boundaries, and don't get mad when people want to encroach on them. Why? Because it is inevitable that people will encroach. Simply state your boundaries clearly and politely, and then stand firm. Go ahead, give it a try. Your doorkeeper and concierge have permission to create the room of your dreams.

## Make Space for Virtual Mentors

You can't achieve harmony unless you are living your current or aspirational values. Virtual mentors in your room help you achieve those aspirational values. Even though physical mentors are outstanding, sometimes they are not enough. As proponents of lifelong learning, we believe a room full of harmony includes space for personal and professional development. Sometimes you have to look beyond who is already in your room and the people waiting to get in and instead seek out virtual mentors, particularly those related to your aspirational goals and values. A virtual mentor is anyone you learn from outside a face-to-face environment. They can be found in books, podcasts, blogs, and online videos. We encourage you to take a moment to think about which of your values are aspirational, and then jot down a list of whom or what you need, such as a certain type of knowledge or skills, to get closer to living a life that reflects those values. This process of reflection helps you identify the types of virtual mentors who will benefit you and allow you to achieve the life you want. Nothing can replace a real mentor in your room. However, virtual mentors can also aid in the intentional design of your room, and these mentors will impact you in ways you can't even imagine now.

Living in harmony inherently means freeing yourself from any guilt you might feel for choosing one activity over another or one person over another. Guilt is an obstacle to harmony. Box up your guilt, and toss it up to the highest shelf in your room.

The concept of the room is about going from the unconscious to the conscious process of decision-making—and we've given you a framework to reset your mindset to consciously build the life you want that is full of harmony instead of just letting it happen.

The truth is that when you are seventy years old, you are not going to wish you had spent more time doing things you didn't like or being with people you didn't enjoy spending time with. Rather than striving for the constantly out-of-reach balance, focus on creating harmony in your room. Be creative. Find ideas that work for you and the life you live. Make the time and be innovative. Balance may be elusive, but harmony is possible. Harmony is created where harmony is sought.

The idea behind "Who's in your room?" allows you to create space for fulfillment. We have written at length about the toxic people in your room since they take up so much space and you have to deal with them. But this is not a negative metaphor. When you move bad relationships farther away, you open up to spending more time and attention on good relationships. When you are deliberate about whom you let into your room and when and why, you become more available to the people who need and love you.

Including yourself.

Remember: you are the curator of your room.

➤ Here's the last exercise: Visualize your room again. Make it as clear as possible and see yourself there. If you like, draw your room or write down its physical characteristics. You might think of it as a simple empty room or a beach or canyon that can be accessed through only one door. Your room might change physically over time, but remember, that door still says "NO EXIT." Note the ways in which your room has changed through the considerations, exercises, and stories in this book. Imagine your new posture and behavior in this room.

How does it feel to be in that room? Let that feeling guide you to greater harmony in every corner of your life.

# Notes

## Chapter 1

9     "Overcoming Trauma & Grief: Eliminate the Hurts That Haunt You," Amen Clinics, October 26, 2018, https://www .amenclinics.com/blog/overcoming-trauma-grief-eliminate -the-hurts-that-haunt-you/.

9     Ben Panko, "How Your Brain Recognizes All Those Faces," *Smithsonian Magazine*, June 6, 2017, smithsonianmag.com /science-nature/how-does-your-brain-recognize-faces -180963583/.

11     Carol Dweck, *Mindset: The New Psychology of Success* (New York: Random House, 2006).

16     For the list of the top five regrets, see Bronnie Ware, "The Top Five Regrets of the Dying," *Bronnie Ware* (blog), bronnieware.com/regrets-of-the-dying/.

17     Gil Bailie, *Violence Unveiled: Humanity at the Crossroads* (New York: Crossroad, 1995), xv.

## Chapter 2

34     For more about Barnet Bain and his work, see Barnet Bain, "Creativity: Resilience in Chaos," *Barnet Bain* (blog), barnetbain.onlinepresskit247.com/.

39     For more information about Geneen Roth's work, see geneenroth.com.

40     Mary Oliver, "When Death Comes," Library of Congress, loc.gov/programs/poetry-and-literature/poet-laureate

/poet-laureate-projects/poetry-180/all-poems/item/poetry
-180-102/when-death-comes/. Originally published in *New
and Selected Poems: Volume One* (Boston: Beacon, 1992).

## Chapter 3

49   Jeffrey D. Johnson et al., "Recollection, Familiarity, and
Cortical Reinstatement: A Multivoxel Pattern Analysis,"
*Neuron* 63, no. 5, (September 2009): 697–708, doi.org
/10.1016/j.neuron.2009.08.011.

51   To watch Matt's TEDx speech, see Matt Weinstein
(speaker), "How to Have More Fun in Your Life," TEDx,
Livermore, California, January 20, 2015, youtube.com
/watch?v=TXwH3SIF9rc.

## Chapter 4

60   Carol Dweck, *Mindset: The New Psychology of Success*
(New York: Random House, 2006).

## Chapter 5

88   Judith Martin, Nicholas Martin, and Jacobina Martin, "Miss
Manners: Conventional Excuses Are Not the Same as Lies,"
*Washington Post*, October 9, 2016, washingtonpost.com
/lifestyle/style/miss-manners-conventional-excuses-are-not
-the-same-as-lies/2016/10/06/a395a73c-81c9-11e6-b002
-307601806392_story.html.

## Chapter 6

97   Hiroyuki Nakao, Isao Ukai, and Joji Kotani, "A Review of
the History of the Origin of Triage from a Disaster Medicine

Perspective," *Acute Medicine and Surgery* 4, no. 4 (July 2017): 379–384, doi.org/10.1002/ams2.293.

107  For more information on Lynne Twist and her books, see soulofmoney.org/.

## Chapter 7

111  "Einstein Sees Boston; Fails on Edison Test; Asked to Tell Speed of Sound He Refers Questioner to Text Books," *New York Times*, May 18, 1921, nytimes.com/1921/05/18 /archives/einstein-sees-boston-fails-on-edison-test-asked -to-tell-speed-of.html.

112  Robin Dunbar, "Dunbar's Number: Why My Theory That Humans Can Only Maintain 150 Friendships Has Withstood 30 Years of Scrutiny," *Conversation*, May 12, 2021, theconversation.com/dunbars-number-why-my-theory-that -humans-can-only-maintain-150-friendships-has-withstood -30-years-of-scrutiny-160676.

119  You can find Stephen at stephenjosephs.com.

## Chapter 8

130  Og Mandino, *The Greatest Secret in the World* (New York: Bantam, 1972), 11.

131  Muhammad Ali, *The Soul of A Butterfly: Reflections on Life's Journey* (New York: Simon & Schuster, 2004).

136  This sentiment is fairly close to our theme that you become whom you're with. Kevin Kelly, "103 Bits of Advice I Wish I Had Known," *Technium*, April 22, 2022, kk.org /thetechnium/103-bits-of-advice-i-wish-i-had-known/.

142  Vivek Murthy and Richard Davidson, interview by Krista Tippett, "The Future of Well-Being," *On Being with Krista Tippett*, December 2, 2021, onbeing.org/programs/vivek -murthy-and-richard-davidson-the-future-of-well-being/.

# Chapter 9

155    "Introduction to the Eight Concepts," Bowen Center for the Study of the Family, accessed June 30, 2022, thebowencenter .org/introduction-eight-concepts.

163    Joe Pinsker, "The Dark Side of Saying, Work Is 'Like a Family,'" *Atlantic*, February 16, 2022, theatlantic.com/family /archive/2022/02/work-actually-is-like-a-family/622813/.

165    Shakespeare, *Hamlet*, act 2, scene 2; Shakespeare, *As You Like It*, act 2, scene 1.

166    Cynthia James's books, online courses, and other services can be found at cynthiajames.net.

# Chapter 10

174    Maurice Eisenberg, "Casals at 70: Great Spanish Cellist Waits for Country's Liberation," *New York Times*, December 29, 1946, nytimes.com/1946/12/29/archives/casals-at-70 -great-spanish-cellist-waits-for-countrys-liberation.html.

180    Examples include *Be Here Now*, *The Power of Now*, and *Wherever You Go, There You Are*.

# Index

# About the Authors

**STEWART EMERY** is cofounder and president of Belvedere Consultants, a boutique consulting firm located in the San Francisco Bay Area. Belvedere supports individuals and organizations in turning their talent into world-class performance and enduring success. Core competencies include designing coherent organizational cultures to deliver extraordinary customer experiences, executive-leadership-team development, radical mentoring and executive performance coaching.

He was one of the creators of the iconic MasterCard "Priceless" campaign. Stewart is coauthor of the international bestseller *Success Built to Last*. He has a lifetime of experience as an entrepreneur, executive coach, and leader and is considered a thought leader of the human potential movement. Stewart has served as a visiting professor at the John F. Kennedy University School of Management and led programs at the Stanford Graduate School of Business. Over the last fifteen years Stewart has led thousands of employees and hundreds of managers around the world through vision, values, strategy, and leadership initiatives based on the research from the international bestsellers *Built to Last* (Collins and Porras), *Good to Great* (Collins), and *Success Built to Last* (Porras, Emery, and Thompson). This body of work is developed from the most comprehensive research project ever undertaken into what makes a great company great, how good companies become great, and the traits of the enduringly successful leaders who build great companies. Stewart has led workshops and seminars and delivered keynotes all over the world.

His bestselling book *Do You Matter? How Great Design Will Make People Love Your Company* was released in September 2008. Coauthored with iconic designer Robert Brunner, who founded Apple's legendary Industrial Design Group and hired Jony Ive, it is considered a business book that does matter.

A wonderful storyteller with a great sense of humor, Stewart has appeared as a featured guest on television and radio talk shows. He has conducted coaching interviews with more than twelve thousand people in the last three decades.

Stewart studied economics, philosophy, and psychology at the University of Sydney before pursuing a career in the advertising arts. He served as a creative director for J. Walter Thompson's Sydney office and taught design at the University of New South Wales. He cofounded Knockout Productions, an award-winning television and radio commercial production company before moving to the United States in 1971.

Stewart settled in the San Francisco Bay Area to pursue his fascination with the psychology of greatness and became passionately engaged in leading workshops and seminars. He was a founding member of est (now Landmark Worldwide) and served as its first CEO. In 1975 Stewart Emery cofounded

Actualizations, an international learning and development organization. In the late '70s he was selected by the national media as one of the ten most influential people in the human potential movement. He has been awarded a doctor of humane letters degree by John F. Kennedy University as an acknowledgment of his contributions.

Stewart's portfolio of passions includes aviation (he and his wife, Joan, are both instrument-rated pilots and fly a Beechcraft Bonanza), coffee, food, jazz, baroque music, travel, and technology. He and Joan live by the San Francisco Bay.

**DR. IVAN MISNER** is the founder and chief visionary officer of BNI, the world's largest business networking organization. Founded in 1985, the organization now has over ten thousand chapters throughout every populated continent of the world. In 2020, BNI generated 11.5 million referrals, resulting in more than $16.2 billion dollars' worth of business for its members.

Dr. Misner's doctorate is from the University of Southern California. He is a *New York Times* bestselling author who has written twenty-six books. He is also a columnist for Entrepreneur.com and has been a university professor as well as a member of the board of trustees for the University of La Verne.

Called the "Father of Modern Networking" by both *Forbes* and CNN, Ivan is considered to be one of the world's leading experts on business networking and has been a keynote speaker for major corporations and associations throughout the world. He has been featured in the *Los Angeles Times*, *Wall Street Journal*, and *New York Times* as well as numerous television and radio shows on CNN and the BBC and the *Today* show on NBC.

Among his many awards, he has been named "Humanitarian of the Year" by the Red Cross and has been the recipient of the John C. Maxwell Leadership Award. He is proud that he and his late wife, Elisabeth, are the cofounders of the BNI Charitable Foundation. They also reached empty-nester status after happily raising their three children. In his spare time, Ivan is also an amateur magician, and he has a black belt in karate.

**DOUG HARDY** creates thought leadership programs for corporate, educational, and private clients. Doug has worked for decades as a writer and collaborator on topics including business management, psychology, technology, history, higher education, and careers. A former executive, he is especially expert on changes to organizations at the nexus of human capital management; technology; well-being; diversity, inclusion, and belonging; and corporate culture. His thought leadership clients include individuals in industries as diverse as management consulting, software, industrial technology, commercial architecture, media, and the history of technology.

Doug is a partner at Hardy, June, & Moore, a nonfiction book agency representing authors of books on business, culture, and personal development (hardyjunemoore.com).

Prior to writing full-time, Doug was a senior media executive running editorial operations in books, magazines, multimedia, and digital content at leading companies like the *New York Times*, Random House, AT&T News Media, and Monster.com. *Who's in Your Room?* is his eighteenth book.

Doug's portfolio of books and other writing is at douglashardy.com.

## Berrett–Koehler
## BK Publishers

**Berrett-Koehler** is an independent publisher dedicated to an ambitious mission: *Connecting people and ideas to create a world that works for all.*

Our publications span many formats, including print, digital, audio, and video. We also offer online resources, training, and gatherings. And we will continue expanding our products and services to advance our mission.

We believe that the solutions to the world's problems will come from all of us, working at all levels: in our society, in our organizations, and in our own lives. Our publications and resources offer pathways to creating a more just, equitable, and sustainable society. They help people make their organizations more humane, democratic, diverse, and effective (and we don't think there's any contradiction there). And they guide people in creating positive change in their own lives and aligning their personal practices with their aspirations for a better world.

And we strive to practice what we preach through what we call "The BK Way." At the core of this approach is *stewardship,* a deep sense of responsibility to administer the company for the benefit of all of our stakeholder groups, including authors, customers, employees, investors, service providers, sales partners, and the communities and environment around us. Everything we do is built around stewardship and our other core values of *quality, partnership, inclusion,* and *sustainability.*

This is why Berrett-Koehler is the first book publishing company to be both a B Corporation (a rigorous certification) and a benefit corporation (a for-profit legal status), which together require us to adhere to the highest standards for corporate, social, and environmental performance. And it is why we have instituted many pioneering practices (which you can learn about at www.bkconnection.com), including the Berrett-Koehler Constitution, the Bill of Rights and Responsibilities for BK Authors, and our unique Author Days.

We are grateful to our readers, authors, and other friends who are supporting our mission. We ask you to share with us examples of how BK publications and resources are making a difference in your lives, organizations, and communities at www.bkconnection.com/impact.

Dear reader,

Thank you for picking up this book and welcome to the worldwide BK community! You're joining a special group of people who have come together to create positive change in their lives, organizations, and communities.

## What's BK all about?

Our mission is to connect people and ideas to create a world that works for all.

Why? Our communities, organizations, and lives get bogged down by old paradigms of self-interest, exclusion, hierarchy, and privilege. But we believe that can change. That's why we seek the leading experts on these challenges—and share their actionable ideas with you.

## A welcome gift

To help you get started, we'd like to offer you a **free copy** of one of our bestselling ebooks:

### www.bkconnection.com/welcome

When you claim your **free ebook**, you'll also be subscribed to our blog.

## Our freshest insights

Access the best new tools and ideas for leaders at all levels on our blog at ideas.bkconnection.com.

Sincerely,

Your friends at Berrett-Koehler

Certified

Corporation